100 MUST-READ
CLASSIC NOVELS

Nick Rennison

A & C Black • London

First published 2006
Reprinted 2007
A & C Black Publishers Limited
38 Soho Square
London W1D 3HB
www.acblack.com

© 2006 Nick Rennison

ISBN-13: 978-0-7136-7583-2

A CIP catalogue record for this book is available from the
British Library.

This book is produced using paper that is made from wood grown in
managed, sustainable forests. It is natural, renewable and recyclable.
The logging and manufacturing processes conform to the environmental
regulations of the country of origin.

Cover design by Jocelyn Lucas

Typeset in 8.5pt on 12pt Meta-Light

Printed in the UK by CPI Bookmarque, Croydon, CR0 4TD

CONTENTS

ABOUTTHISBOOK

This book is not intended to provide a list of the 100 'best' novels ever published. Given the sheer range of 'classic' fiction and the unpredictability of individual taste, any such definitive list is an impossibility. It may just be possible to agree on the indisputable greatness of a handful of novels (*War and Peace* is an example), although even then the chances are that there will be a few maverick voices raised in opposition, but a longer list is bound to cause debate. In the end, my choice was guided by the title of the book. I have chosen 100 books to read which I think will provide some sense of the enormous range of fiction, from the adventures of a would-be knight errant in 17th-century Spain to the narrative of an alienated man's crimes in 20th-century Algeria, that can be described as 'classic'.

The entries are arranged A to Z by author. They describe the plot of each title (while aiming to avoid too many 'spoilers'), offer some value judgements and say something briefly about the author's place in the history of literature and/or their other works. I have noted significant film versions (with dates of release) where applicable, followed by 'Read On' lists comprised of books by the same author, books by stylistically similar writers or books on a theme relevant to the main entry. I have also included a number of 'Read on a Theme' lists which are scattered throughout the text after appropriate titles. The symbol ❯❯ before an author name (e.g. ❯❯ Charles Dickens) indicates that one or more of their books is covered in the A to Z author entries.

Although the blurb-writers of many modern novels would have us believe otherwise, an instant classic is pretty much a contradiction in terms – part of the process by which a book attains classic status involves the passage of time. In picking a list of classics, some kind of cut-off date is needed. In a sense, any date selected (1939? 1945? 1960?) would be an arbitrary one, but I decided eventually on 1950. It is a conveniently rounded figure and it means that the passage of more than a half a century has provided time for a variety of assessments of a particular work to be made and its merits as a potential 'classic' to be widely discussed. All the books chosen were published before that date. (The date attached to each first choice book in the guide refers to the first publication of the novel in book form.) All books in the Read on a Theme menus were also published before 1950 but, in the Read Ons to individual entries, I have allowed myself to choose titles that first appeared after 1950 as well as before.

Most authors receive one entry only. The original intention was to have 100 authors and 100 books but it soon became clear that this was impractical. How can the richness and variety of authors like Dickens, Dostoevsky and Hardy be represented by only one book? How can *Anna Karenina* be included in a list of 100 must-read classics and *War and Peace* be excluded? Or vice versa? Yet, if every masterpiece by a dozen or so writers were to be included, there would be room for very few other authors. In the end, I decided (again, more or less arbitrarily) that the most any author could have would be two titles.

I have ignored the constraints of the title in one instance only. It seems to me that Chekhov is, indisputably, one of the greatest, most insightful and most humane writers of fiction in history, but his fiction consists almost exclusively of short stories. His early narrative, *The Shooting Party*, is a novel by most definitions of the word but it is not his best work and it seemed to me perverse to choose it in preference to the short stories. In the end I decided to stretch a point and include his *Selected Short Stories* among the 100 Must-Read Classic Novels.

INTRODUCTION

What is a classic? Is it, as the dictionary defines it, 'a standard work, one of established excellence and quality'? Was the American critic Alfred Kazin right (if a bit pompous) when he described a classic as 'a book that survives the circumstances that made it possible yet alone keeps these circumstances alive?' There are, thankfully, other definitions available. For some of us, a classic is simply a fat book we've taken on holiday and not read. It may come in various versions. There is the Russian version, which contains so many characters with so many names, some of which seem to be arbitrarily interchangeable, that the reader's head is spinning after a couple of chapters. There is the French version which is always about adultery. There is the English version, often written by a severe-looking Victorian gentleman with the kind of beard in which birds can nest unnoticed. Whatever the version, we have all had the experience of packing a hefty Penguin Classic in our suitcase, virtuously intent on polishing off ›› Proust or *War and Peace* on the beach, only to return with the book and its pages scarcely disturbed. More than a hundred years ago, ›› Mark Twain wrote that, 'A classic is something that everybody wants to have read and nobody wants to read.' His words, often enough, still hold true today.

For the book snob, a classic means something else. It's a weapon that he (and it's usually he) can wield in the war to prove that he's cleverer than everyone else. With that sneer that says, 'Surely you must have read that, haven't you?' forever on his face, he's always several steps ahead of the rest of us. The book snob has read *Don Quixote* four times, twice in the original Castilian. He's ploughed his way through *Moby Dick* and *The Brothers Karamazov* without skipping the dull bits. He knows classics in languages like Serbo-Croat and Farsi which we didn't know even possessed classics. It's little use trying to compete with him. Even if, by some small miracle, we have read *War and Peace* on the beach and want to boast about it, the book snob thinks it's much over-rated and prefers an earlier novel by ›› Tolstoy that has only ever been translated once, in 1903, and has been out of print since ›› Graham Greene was in short trousers.

For the literary academic, on the other hand, the classic represents a job opportunity. All those novels that are set on literature courses throughout the land need a full-scale critical apparatus to support them. They need introductions and notes and plot summaries and character analyses. These are not books that can be just read. They require experts to guide us through them. When ›› Dickens writes about a one-legged man, it is assumed that we would be lost without extensive footnotes which chronicle the history of the wooden leg from Roman times to the Victorian era, describe methods of amputation in 19th-century England, list the other uniped characters in Dickens's novels and speculate wildly about the psychological meaning of the author's interest in limb loss. There is no shortage of assistant lecturers in literature and cultural studies prepared to step up to the mark and provide them.

This book has been compiled with a different view of 'classics' in mind. These are books that don't always need scholarly introductions. They don't always need to be supported by a vast scaffolding of notes and references. We shouldn't try to read them as an act of masochistic duty on some Mediterranean beach nor use them as gambling chips in a game of literary oneupmanship. Books like *War and Peace*, *Great Expectations* and *Madame Bovary* (all included in this guide) deserve to be read because they are at least as vivid and exciting and entertaining as the most contemporary of bestsellers and usually more so.

I have tried to make the selection of 100 titles as interesting and varied as I could. There are some books and authors that selected themselves. What guide to classic fiction could possibly exclude Tolstoy or Dickens or ›› George Eliot? Or ›› Jane Austen, ›› Thomas Hardy and ›› James Joyce? However, compiling a list of 100 books allows plenty of scope for more unusual and less well-known titles and writers. ›› Halldór Laxness, ›› Sigrid Undset and ›› Italo Svevo may not be household names, even in literary households (although two of them were awarded the Nobel Prize for Literature), but they are all, in my opinion, great writers and I have taken the opportunity to include novels by them in the book. There is also a tendency to believe that a 'classic' must necessarily be gloomy and tragic in its subject matter. Comic fiction is often seen, by its very nature, to be somehow lightweight. Looking through the list, there is certainly quite a high proportion of novels that look at life with an unflinching awareness of all its miseries, failures and disappointments. However, I see no reason why the brilliance of great comic writing should not be acknowledged and authors like ›› Stella Gibbons, ›› P.G. Wodehouse and ›› Flann O'Brien, in my opinion, more than deserve the status of classics.

In the end, I return to the argument of an earlier paragraph. The best classics shouldn't be slightly scary cultural monuments which, as Twain claimed, everybody wants to have read but nobody wants to read. All the books in this guide, in their very different ways, are worth reading because, as the best fiction should do, they continue to provide exciting ways of entering the emotional experience of a vast range of people from all sorts of countries, backgrounds, periods of history and kinds of society. Whether the world they open up is Russia in the 19th century, Bath in the Regency era, Dublin on 16 June 1904, the American Deep South after the Civil War or London in the 1930s, they give us the pleasures of empathy and enlightenment that good fiction always offers. They provide an enlargement of the necessarily narrow horizons of our own small lives.

A-Z OF ENTRIES

LOUISA MAY ALCOTT (1832–88) USA

LITTLE WOMEN (1868)

The daughter of Bronson Alcott, a renowned American educationalist, Louisa May Alcott published more than two hundred books but is largely remembered for just one – *Little Women*. Following the fortunes of Meg, Jo, Beth and Amy March, the daughters of an army chaplain in the American Civil War, the book records both the everyday pleasures and the trials and tribulations of their lives. Would-be writer Jo has the excitement of getting a story published. The wealthy Mr Laurence and his grandson Laurie become close friends of the family. Laurie's young tutor falls in love with Meg. A telegram arrives with the bad news that Mr March is hospitalized in Washington DC and Mrs March, partly financed by money from the sale of Jo's hair, is obliged to travel there to look after him. As the girls, based on Alcott and her own sisters, progress from teenage years to young womanhood, they face further crisis and tragedy. The saintly Beth contracts scarlet fever while visiting sick neighbours and, as the other girls grow up and face the challenges of work and romance, she has to battle with terminal illness. In later life, Alcott wrote in her journal that she was 'tired of providing moral pap for the young' and published a number of novels which attempted to deal with what she saw as more adult themes, but *Little Women* survives and thrives nearly a century and a half after it was first published precisely because it is much more than just a simplistic morality tale. The novel is set very firmly in the place and period in which it was written – readers can learn much about the social history of mid-19th-century America from reading *Little Women* – but it has a universality that transcends both.

📖 **Film version:** *Little Women* (starring Elizabeth Taylor as Amy and June Allyson as Jo, 1949); *Little Women* (with Winona Ryder as Jo, 1994)

📚 **Read on**
Little Men
Geraldine Brooks, *March* (a modern Pulitzer Prize-winning novel which takes the father of Alcott's March family as its central character); Susan Coolidge, *What Katy Did*; Laura Ingalls Wilder, *The Little House on the Prairie*

JANE AUSTEN (1775–1817) UK

EMMA (1816)

Young, well-off and spoiled, Emma Woodhouse is complacently convinced that she knows what is best for everyone, particularly in matters of the heart. Her matchmaking skills are largely directed towards her young, amiable and innocent *protegée* Harriet Smith, whom Emma decides would be ideally matched with the clergyman, Mr Elton. Elton, however, has other ideas and, despising Harriet for her lack of social status, he has his eye on Emma herself. Emma plays with the idea of being in love with Frank Churchill, recently arrived as a visitor in her village, but her real, unrecognized feelings are for the sympathetic and warm-hearted local squire, George Knightley who watches her attempts to shape other people's lives with a mixture of affection and irritation. As Emma's assorted schemes collapse in embarrassment and, occasionally, distress, she is forced to acknowledge that she knows less about herself and about other people than she once believed she did. 'Three or four families in a country village,' Jane Austen wrote in a letter to one of her relatives, 'is the very thing to work on.' It was the world which she knew intimately herself. Born in a Hampshire village where her father was rector, she spent most of her life in the midst of her family either there or at Chawton, another village in Hampshire, or at Bath. Although she had several suitors, she never married. She died of Addison's disease in Winchester at the age of only 41. All this might suggest that, as a novelist, she worked on a restricted canvas. *Emma*, as much as any of her novels, shows that there is far more to Jane Austen than the image of a rural spinster implies. Her tough-minded realism about human motivation and self-deceit, about the manoeuvrings of the marriage market and the institution of the family give her works a sharpness and a truthfulness all their own.

🍴 **Film versions:** *Emma* (starring Gwyneth Paltrow as Emma, 1996); *Clueless* (a version of the story updated to 1990s Beverley Hills, 1995)

📚 **Read on**
Mansfield Park; *Persuasion*
Joan Aiken, *Mansfield Revisited*; Barbara Pym, *Excellent Women*

PRIDE AND PREJUDICE (1813)

Jane Austen began writing *Pride and Prejudice*, then entitled *First Impressions*, when she was in her early twenties but it was rejected by a publisher and only finally appeared, in a much revised form and under a new title, in 1813. The book focuses on the Bennet family of mother, father and five nubile daughters, thrown into confusion by the arrival of two rich and unattached young men in the neighbourhood. Charles Bingley leases Netherfield, a house close to the Bennet residence and stays there together with his friend Fitzwilliam Darcy. During visits exchanged between the two houses, Bingley falls in love with the eldest Bennet daughter, Jane, while Darcy and Elizabeth, the second eldest, circle one another warily. Witty, clever and ironic, Elizabeth is intrigued by Darcy but dislikes his apparent coldness and arrogance and is prejudiced against him by stories she hears from others. At different times throughout the novel, misunderstandings, social snobbery and self-will conspire to keep both Jane and Bingley and Darcy and

Elizabeth apart. But true love finally triumphs. A supporting cast of characters, often richly comic, orbits the central figures of Darcy and Elizabeth. The ill-matched relationship between the ironic, detached Mr Bennet and his gushing, silly wife is beautifully observed. Lady Catherine de Bourgh is a splendidly self-satisfied and snobbish representative of everything that is bad about the aristocracy. Mr Collins, the clergyman and toady to Lady Catherine, unwittingly reveals himself in his true colours during the memorable scene in which he proposes marriage to Elizabeth. *Pride and Prejudice* has long been Jane Austen's most popular novel and, with its clear-eyed portrait of the ways in which society's conventions dictate the shifting patterns of the relationships between the men and women in it, it is one of the greatest comedies of social manners in English literature.

Film versions: *Pride and Prejudice* (starring Greer Garson as Elizabeth and Laurence Olivier as Darcy,1940); *Pride and Prejudice* (Jennifer Ehle as Elizabeth, Colin Firth as Darcy, 1995, TV); *Pride and Prejudice* (Keira Knightley as Elizabeth, Mathew Macfadyen as Darcy, 2005)

⮞ Read on
Sense and Sensibility
>> Elizabeth Gaskell, *Wives and Daughters*; Alison Lurie, *Only Children*; Emma Tennant, *Pemberley* (a sequel, published in 1993); Joanna Trollope, *Other People's Children*; Fay Weldon, *Letters to Alice on First Reading Jane Austen*

READONATHEME: THREE OR FOUR FAMILIES IN A COUNTRY VILLAGE

>> Jane Austen, *Emma*
>> Elizabeth Gaskell, *Cranford*
   Oliver Goldsmith, *The Vicar of Wakefield*
   F.M. Mayor, *The Rector's Daughter*
   Barbara Pym, *Some Tame Gazelle*
   Flora Thompson, *Lark Rise to Candleford*
>> Anthony Trollope, *Framley Parsonage*

HONORÉ DE BALZAC (1799–1850) France

EUGÉNIE GRANDET (1833)

Balzac began his career as a novelist with pseudonymously published historical novels in imitation of >> Sir Walter Scott but, as he turned to fiction with a contemporary setting, he gradually evolved a grandly ambitious plan to write a series of novels which would provide a panoramic portrait of French society in the first half of the 19th century. *La Comédie Humaine* (*The Human Comedy*), as he entitled the whole project, was never finished but, even so, it runs to more than 90 individual but interconnected works of fiction which together include thousands of characters. *Eugénie Grandet*, one of the earliest novels in the series, is set in the stifling household of Monsieur Grandet, a wealthy but miserly wine merchant in the French provincial town of Saumur. Grandet controls the life of his submissive and naïve daughter, Eugénie, whom he plans to marry off to his advantage rather than hers; she, however, falls in love with her penniless cousin Charles. But Charles proves as worthless a man as her father. Despatched to the West Indies to make his fortune, he soon forgets his promises to Eugénie and when he returns, rich from dealings in the slave trade, he chooses to marry for social position rather than love. Eugénie's hopes for emotional fulfilment have been ruined by the greed of both her father and her one-time suitor. Balzac's huge cycle of novels contains many other brilliant depictions of everyday tragedies like Eugénie's. *Old Goriot*, for example, tells the Lear-like story of an old man living in a down-at-heel Parisian boarding house who sacrifices his all for his two married daughters. In return they treat him with contempt and offhand neglect. However, none of Balzac's books possesses quite the power to touch and move the reader as *Eugénie Grandet*, with its tale of blighted love and the baleful power of money.

≋ Read on

Cousin Bette; *Old Goriot*
Theodore Dreiser; *An American Tragedy*; ›› Henry James, *Washington Square*; François Mauriac, *A Woman of the Pharisees*; ›› Émile Zola, *Nana*

ARNOLD BENNETT (1867–1931) UK

THE OLD WIVES' TALE (1908)

Arnold Bennett was born in Hanley, one of the Staffordshire Potteries towns in which he set much of his fiction. Some of the many novels he published from the 1890s until his death do move outside the Potteries. *Riceyman Steps*, for example, is set in Clerkenwell, London and scrutinizes, with cruelly clinical detachment, the life of the miserly Henry Earlforward, who inherits a secondhand bookshop and enters, in middle age, upon the courtship of a widow who has moved into a nearby shop. However, despite the fact that Bennett himself became very much a metropolitan man, at home amid the great and good of literary and artistic London, his most characteristic novels remain those in which he reconstructed the provincial world of his boyhood. Of these, the most rewarding for the reader is probably *The Old Wives' Tale*, which focuses on two sisters, the daughters of a prosperous draper in the Five Towns, who lead contrasting but equally difficult lives. Constance, as her name suggests, is the stay-at-home sister who marries her father's apprentice and settles into a life of conventional motherhood and routine domesticity. Sophia, less easily satisfied with what the Potteries have to offer, elopes to Paris with a caddish charmer named Gerald Scales. There Scales deserts her and she is forced to endure the hardships of the siege that the city endures after the Franco-Prussian War and to struggle to find a new place in the world. The novel follows the sisters throughout their lives until the twists and turns of fate return both of them, as old women, to their childhood home. Bennett revisited the Potteries in an even more ambitious sequence of novels beginning with *Clayhanger*, in 1910, which charts the life and career of its eponymous hero Edwin Clayhanger, but *The Old Wives' Tale* is as powerful and moving a piece of social realism as he ever wrote.

🕮 **Read on**

Anna of the Five Towns; *Clayhanger*; *Riceyman Steps*
Theodore Dreiser, *Sister Carrie*; ▶▶ D.H. Lawrence, *The Rainbow*; ▶▶
H.G. Wells, *Ann Veronica*

READONATHEME: LIFE IN THE PROVINCES

There is a world outside London
    William Cooper, *Scenes From Provincial Life*
    A.J. Cronin, *The Stars Look Down*
▶▶ George Eliot, *Middlemarch*
▶▶ Elizabeth Gaskell, *Sylvia's Lovers*
    Winifred Holtby, *South Riding*
▶▶ D.H. Lawrence, *The Rainbow*
    Richard Llewellyn, *How Green Was My Valley*
    Howard Spring, *Shabby Tiger*

ELIZABETH BOWEN (1899–1973) Ireland

THE DEATH OF THE HEART (1938)

Born into the Anglo-Irish gentry (her family home was Bowen's Court, near Dublin), Elizabeth Bowen set her finest works not in Ireland but in London. *The Heat of the Day*, for example, is one of the most effective of all evocations of London in the Blitz and examines the love affair of Stella Rodney and Robert Kelway, doomed by both the large-scale upheaval in which it is conducted and by the sinister machinations of Stella's other suitor who betrays the fact that Kelway is a spy. As the plot moves towards its inevitable and foreshadowed conclusion, the themes of love and betrayal play themselves out against the backdrop of a city at war, one in which all the characters seem to have lost their bearings. In *The Death of the Heart*, published in the late 1930s, Portia Quayne is an innocent abroad in the deracinated world of metropolitan sophisticates. Orphaned by the death of her mother, with whom she had been leading a peripatetic life in assorted hotels on the Continent, the sixteen-year-old Portia is taken in by her wealthy half-brother and his wife who live in some style in fashionable London. All three of them find the new arrangements difficult but it is when Portia's naïvely insightful diary falls into the hands of her sister-in-law Anna and when the young girl believes herself to have fallen in love with Eddie, a vain and self-centred admirer of Anna, that trouble really begins. Finally, Portia flees her half-brother's house and takes refuge in a residential hotel in Kensington. Curiously, Elizabeth Bowen did not like her own novel overmuch and she once dismissed it as 'an inflated short story'. Today its tragicomic portrait of a vulnerable young girl bemused by the new world into which she is thrust seems far more powerful and perceptive than its author was prepared to acknowledge.

🕮 Read on
The Heat of the Day; *The Last September*
›› Henry James, *What Maisie Knew*; William Trevor, *Mrs Eckdorf in O'Neill's Hotel*; Angus Wilson, *The Middle Age of Mrs Eliot*

CHARLOTTE BRONTË (1816–55) UK

JANE EYRE (1847)
The history of the Brontë family, with its record of illness, alcoholism, unrequited loves and early deaths, is as compelling as any of the books written by the Brontë sisters. All three sisters published their first novels in 1847. Anne's story was *Agnes Grey* and ›› Emily's *Wuthering Heights*. Charlotte, the eldest of the three, made her debut with *Jane Eyre*, in which a young governess falls in love with her brooding employer but cannot marry him because of the dark secrets from his past that still haunt him. The narrative follows its eponymous heroine from her orphaned childhood and her miserable experience of institutional life at Lowood Asylum, alleviated only briefly by her doomed friendship with the gentle Helen Burns, to her young adulthood as a governess. Despatched to Thornfield Hall to tutor the ward of its master, Edward

Rochester, Jane finds herself drawn to her enigmatic employer and he is attracted by her quiet but determined character. A marriage is all set to take place when word reaches Jane that Rochester is married already. Indeed his wife, a violent lunatic, is incarcerated in the attic of Thornfield Hall itself. The wedding, of course, is cancelled and the would-be bride and groom have to go their separate ways. Reduced to near destitution, Jane is finally taken in by the virtuous and compassionate St Rivers family. Only after many more twists and turns of fate, some more improbable than others, are she and Rochester brought together again and the obstacles that stand in the way of their love removed. Charlotte Brontë's novel, one of the most famous of the 19th century, transcends the romantic melodrama and often absurd coincidences of its plot to show readers the slow emotional progress of its heroine and the gradual maturing of her personality under pressure.

◤ **Film versions:** *Jane Eyre* (Orson Welles as Rochester and Joan Fontaine as Jane, 1944); *Jane Eyre* (directed by Franco Zeffirelli, with William Hurt and Charlotte Gainsbourg, 1996)

▧ Read on
The Professor; *Shirley*
Daphne Du Maurier, *Rebecca*; ▸▸ George Eliot, *The Mill on the Floss*; Jean Rhys, *Wide Sargasso Sea* (a novel which recreates the past life of the first Mrs Rochester, the madwoman in the attic)

EMILY BRONTË (1818–48) UK

WUTHERING HEIGHTS (1847)

The half-wild foundling Heathcliff, introduced as a child into the Earnshaw family, falls in love with Cathy Earnshaw as they grow up but any chance of future happiness together is thwarted by Cathy's own ambivalent feelings (she is strongly attracted to Heathcliff yet feels that marriage to him would be socially impossible) and by the fierce antagonism of Hindley, Cathy's brother. Heathcliff chooses exile rather than the humiliation of staying at Wuthering Heights and disappears abroad. When he returns, he discovers that Cathy has married a neighbour, Edgar Linton. The rest of the novel chronicles Heathcliff's terrible vengeance on the Earnshaws and the Lintons for the wrongs he believes they have done him, a vengeance that echoes down the generations, long after Heathcliff himself is dead. Cathy dies in childbirth, driven to despair by the consequences of her choice of social convention over passion when she married Linton rather than Heathcliff, and by the mental torment Heathcliff inflicts on her. Isabella Linton, Edgar's sister, falls in love with Heathcliff and marries him but he uses her only as a means of gaining power over the rest of her family. Hindley succumbs to drink and dissipation and Wuthering Heights, which he had inherited from his father, falls into Heathcliff's hands. The next generation (Hindley's son Hareton, Catherine's daughter and Linton, Heathcliff's and Isabella's child) have the sins of their fathers and their mothers visited upon them and struggle to escape the consequences. Contemporaries were astonished and disconcerted by the raw emotion of Emily Brontë's novel when it first appeared in 1847, the year before her early death from TB, and it has continued to enthral readers in the century and a half since that first publication. Melodramatic and wildly romantic the doomed love story of Cathy and Heathcliff may be but it has lost none of its power to stir the imagination.

▰ Film versions: *Wuthering Heights* (Merle Oberon as Cathy and Laurence Olivier as Heathcliff, 1939); *Wuthering Heights* (Juliette Binoche as Cathy and Ralph Fiennes as Heathcliff, 1992)

⮔ Read on

R.D. Blackmore, *Lorna Doone*; Anne Brontë, *The Tenant of Wildfell Hall*; Daphne Du Maurier, *My Cousin Rachel*; ❯❯ Thomas Hardy, *Tess of the D'Urbervilles*

SAMUEL BUTLER (1835–1902) UK

THE WAY OF ALL FLESH (1903)

Poet, painter, musician, critic, amateur scientist and philosopher, Samuel Butler was a polymathic but faintly ridiculous figure in late 19th-century culture, as likely to pursue eccentric hobbyhorses (his belief that Homer was a woman, for example) as he was to produce significant works of literature. However, *Erewhon*, his satirical novel about a society where Victorian values were turned on their heads, remains brilliantly readable and *The Way of All Flesh*, published posthumously, is a powerful fictional critique of the orthodoxies of the age. The novel charts several generations of a family but it focuses on Ernest Pontifex whose anxious and unhappy character is shaped by the narrow religious beliefs of his father and grandfather before him. Ordained as a minister more because his family wishes it than because he has any genuine vocation for the church, Ernest faces social catastrophe when he naïvely mistakes a respectable woman for a prostitute and propositions her. He is imprisoned but, ironically, this proves a liberating experience, allowing him to begin the process of shaking off the shackles of religious and social conformity which bind him. More trials and tribulations are to follow – he enters unwittingly into a bigamous marriage with a former chambermaid, for example – but he is on the road to self-fulfilment. *The Way of All Flesh* was written more than twenty years before Butler's death but he chose not to publish it in his lifetime. When it did appear it was immediately hailed as a devastating assault on the hypocrisies and self-righteousness of the Victorian age. Reaching for hyperbole, George Bernard Shaw called it 'one of the summits of human achievement'. For modern readers it can have little of the revelatory power it had for its first audience but it remains a witty and compassionate exploration of religious and social repression and of one man's struggle to attain his true self.

⮒ Read on

Erewhon

Ivy Compton-Burnett, *A House and Its Head*; Edmund Gosse, *Father and Son* (autobiography rather than fiction but a similar portrait of incompatability of beliefs across the Victorian generations)

ALBERT CAMUS (1913–60) Algeria/France

THE OUTSIDER (1942)

Of Nobel Prize winners in literature only ➤➤ Rudyard Kipling was younger than Camus was when he received the award in 1957. According to the judges, he received the prize for work which 'illuminates the problems of the human conscience in our times'. This work ranges from *The Plague*, a novel set in a quarantined North African town, and *The Fall*, the record of one man's disillusionment with the life he had been leading, to plays and philosophical essays such as *The Rebel* and *The Myth of Sisyphus*. His best known and most widely read book, however, is *The Outsider*, sometimes translated, more accurately, as *The Stranger*. Set in Algeria, the country in which Camus grew up, the novel focuses on the alienated figure of Meursault. At the beginning of the novel he has just received word of his mother's death ('Mother died today. Or yesterday maybe, I don't know' are the famous opening lines which establish very concisely Meursault's detachment from everyday emotions) and he is about to travel to her funeral. The narrative follows the next few days in Meursault's life, culminating in his shooting of a man on a heat-ravaged beach. As the law moves into action to deal with

Meursault's crime, attention focuses as much on his apparent indifference to his mother's death and on his unsettling beliefs about the essential meaninglessness of life as on the murder he committed. Albert Camus died in a car crash three years after becoming a Nobel Laureate. The legacy he left consists of the writings, both fictional and non-fictional, in which he presents his vision of an absurd universe where man can only assert his freedom and individuality by coming to recognize that rationality and meaning in life are unattainable goals. Of these writings, *The Outsider* continues to be the most accessible and the most rewarding for readers.

📽 **Film version:** *Lo Straniero* (directed by Luchino Visconti, with Marcello Mastroianni as Meursault, 1967)

📖 **Read on**
The Fall; *The Plague*
Saul Bellow, *The Victim*; André Gide, *The Immoralist*; ›› Victor Hugo, *The Last Day of a Man Condemned to Death*; Jean Paul Sartre, *Nausea*

LEWIS CARROLL (1832–98) UK

ALICE'S ADVENTURES IN WONDERLAND (1865)

Lewis Carroll was the pseudonym chosen by Charles Lutwidge Dodgson when he decided to publish the stories he had been inventing to amuse Alice Liddell, the young daughter of the Dean of Christ Church, Oxford. *Alice's Adventures in Wonderland*, originally published as *Alice's Adventures Under Ground*, begins when the heroine of the title, out on a picnic, tumbles down a rabbit hole into a world turned upside down. Different potions make her grow and shrink in size. She meets with a baby that metamorphoses into a pig, animals that are more human than most humans and playing cards that come to life and play croquet. Surreal before the word was invented, these fantasies of a shy Oxford mathematics don have become classics of children's literature. Alice's encounters with the Cheshire Cat and the March Hare, her experiences at the Mad Hatter's tea party and her attendance at the trial of the knave of hearts for stealing some tarts liberate the reader's imagination in a way few other works can do. In the years since their publication, they have been subjected to minute examination by critics in search of every kind of interpretation, from psychoanalytical to political, but they remain mysterious and delightfully resistant to ultimate explanation. Six years after the publication of *Alice's Adventures in Wonderland*, Carroll produced a sequel, very nearly as good, entitled *Through the Looking Glass*, in which the young heroine travels to a world behind her mirror where nursery rhyme characters (Humpty Dumpty, Tweedledum and Tweedledee) are living their own strange lives. Crammed with puns and parodies, riddles and logic games, Carroll's two Alice books are unique, utterly unlike any other children's classics, and have influenced writers, artists and musicians from ›› James Joyce and Jorge Luis Borges to John Lennon and the creators of Japanese anime films.

🎬 **Film version:** *Alice in Wonderland* (Disney cartoon version, 1951)

📖 **Read on**
Through the Looking Glass, and What Alice Found There
Edwin Abbott, *Flatland*; Gilbert Adair, *Alice Through the Needle's Eye* (new adventures for Alice by a modern novelist); Kenneth Grahame, *The Wind in the Willows*; ›› Rudyard Kipling, *The Jungle Book*; Charles Kingsley, *The Water Babies*

WILLA CATHER (1876–1947) USA

MY ÁNTONIA (1918)

Willa Cather began her career as a journalist in Pittsburgh and later worked for high-profile New York magazines but, in her thirties, she began to write the novels, largely set in the Midwest she knew from her childhood, which made her name. *O Pioneers!*, for example, is the story of a Swedish immigrant family, the Bergsons, and their struggles to make a living from their prairie farmstead. Her finest and, in many ways, most characteristic novel, *My Ántonia*, has a similar setting. Through the eyes of the narrator Jim Burden, the book tells the life story of Ántonia Shimerda, the eldest daughter of a family of immigrant farmers in Nebraska. Ántonia is a powerful personality – she 'had always been one to leave images in the mind that did not fade', according to Burden – and, in the course of the novel, her strength and determination to survive are severely tested. When she is still only a teenager, her father, homesick and unable to settle in his new country, commits suicide. Forced to work for others, she struggles to retain her independence and her sense of self-worth. As a young woman, an unhappy and ill-fated love affair leaves her with an illegitimate child and a tarnished reputation. Yet when Burden, by now a successful city lawyer, returns after twenty years to visit the land he knew in his childhood, he finds that Ántonia has married a fellow immigrant and is at the centre of a large and happy family. *My Ántonia* is a powerful testament to both the landscape of Nebraska and the people who pioneered its cultivation. It is also a compelling portrait of the enduring friendship between Burden and Ántonia and of Ántonia herself, an apparently ordinary woman who, the novel shows, has extraordinary resilience and determination to make something of her life.

🕮 Read on

Death Comes for the Archbishop; *A Lost Lady*; *O, Pioneers!*
Ellen Glasgow, *Barren Ground*; Sarah Orne Jewett, *The Country of the Pointed Firs*; ➤➤ Edith Wharton, *Ethan Frome*

MIGUEL DE CERVANTES (1547–1616) Spain

DON QUIXOTE (1605 and 1615)

A middle-aged Spanish gentleman from the region of La Mancha, Don Quixote has befuddled his mind with the tales of knightly derring-do and chivalric deeds that he reads. He decides that the world needs a knight errant of the kind that he finds in his books and that he is the man to become one. Riding forth on his steed Rocinante, actually a broken-down nag, and accompanied by his trusty squire, in reality a cheerfully down-to-earth peasant named Sancho Panza, Don Quixote travels through Spain in search of potential glory. His adventures are the result of his persistent misinterpretations, in the light of the stories he has read, of the ordinary events he and Sancho Panza encounter on the road. Famously, he mistakes windmills for giants, and when charging them with his lance brings disaster, he blames the results on a magician who has changed the giants into windmills in order to deprive him of the glory of overcoming them. A funeral procession becomes, in Quixote's mind, a troop of devils carrying off a princess, a barber's basin the miraculous Helmet of Bambrino. All his attempts at living out the dream of chivalry end in humiliation and suffering. Yet the power of Cervantes's narrative lies in the gradual transformation of Don Quixote, during the course of the novel, from a bumbling buffoon into a noble idealist, lost amid the brutal practicalities of the real world. Misguided and deluded though he is, Quixote comes to represent all that is best and honourable in human nature. His defeats are the defeats of our better selves. When Cervantes published *Don Quixote*, chivalric romances to inspire the would-be knight belonged to the past; the future belonged to the kind of narrative that Cervantes himself created. It is one of the first books in the history of world literature that can be properly described as a novel and, nearly four hundred years after it first appeared, it is still one of the greatest.

🎬 **Film version:** *Man of La Mancha* (Hollywood musical version, with Peter O'Toole and Sophia Loren, 1972)

📖 **Read on**
Exemplary Stories
➤➤ Charles Dickens, *The Pickwick Papers*; ➤➤ Henry Fielding, *Tom Jones*; ➤➤ Graham Greene, *Monsignor Quixote*; ➤➤ Jaroslav Hašek, *The Good Soldier Svejk*

ANTON CHEKHOV (1860–1904) Russia

COLLECTED STORIES
'Write as much as you can!' Chekhov once advised a fellow author, 'Write, write, write, until your fingers break.' Although he died of TB when he was still only in his early forties, Chekhov left behind a large body of work. Plays like *The Seagull*, *Uncle Vanya* and *The Cherry Orchard* made him the leading Russian dramatist of his day but he was, for many years, best known for his short stories, of which he wrote

hundreds. In the finest of these, Chekhov presents, with sympathetic detachment, a portrait gallery of ordinary people, with all their everyday loves, losses and dreams of a better life. In 'The Lady with the Dog', a chance meeting on the seafront leads to a short affair and to an older man's realization that he is genuinely in love for the first time in his life. 'On Official Business' shows a young magistrate arriving in a remote village to conduct the inquest into a suicide and reflecting on the frustrations and drudgery of his own life. Chekhov can be more direct in his descriptions of human suffering. In 'Ward No. 6', for example, a savagely ironic tale of role reversals, Dr Rabin, a psychiatrist at a squalid provincial lunatic asylum, is drawn into an ambivalent friendship with one of the inmates. Rabin's own mental health comes under scrutiny and eventually he is tricked into becoming an inmate of his own asylum. However, the typical Chekhov story is restrained and undemonstrative, quietly opening a window on ordinary life and showing, with great subtlety and sophistication, the motives and feelings of his characters, often hidden from themselves as much as they are from other people. Chekhov's influence on the short story in the century since his death has been enormous, and writers as different as the American dirty realist Raymond Carver and the English author V.S. Pritchett acknowledged their debt to him.

⋙ Read on

Raymond Carver, *Where I'm Calling From* (Carver was a great admirer of Chekhov); V.S. Pritchett, *Collected Stories*; ›› Ivan Turgenev, *Sketches from a Hunter's Album*

READ ON A THEME: SHORT STORIES

Ambrose Bierce, *In the Midst of Life*
>> Ernest Hemingway, *Men Without Women*
O. Henry, *Collected Stories*
>> James Joyce, *Dubliners*
>> Rudyard Kipling, *Soldiers Three*
Ring Lardner, *Collected Short Stories*
Katherine Mansfield, *The Garden Party and Other Stories*
>> Guy de Maupassant, *Boule de Suif and Other Stories*
V.S. Pritchett, *Collected Short Stories*
Damon Runyon, *Guys and Dolls*
Saki (H.H. Munro), *Chronicles of Clovis*

KATE CHOPIN (1851–1904) USA

THE AWAKENING (1899)

Married at the age of nineteen to a New Orleans businessman, Kate Chopin only began her writing career after the deaths of her husband and her mother and her own subsequent mental breakdown. Her first novel, *At Fault*, was published in 1890 and was followed by a succession of short stories and articles for a wide variety of monthly magazines. *The Awakening* is by far her best-known work and tells the story of Edna Pontellier, a wife and mother living in some comfort in Louisiana who comes to question the life she is leading. During a summer vacation, her flirtation with the young and romantic Robert Lebrun awakens her to the idea that there may be more to life than social conventions suggest. On her return from vacation to New Orleans she determines to act upon her newly aroused feelings. Working as a painter and selling her paintings gives her a greater sense of independence and she asserts this further by moving out of the family home and engaging in a brief affair with a charming but egotistical womanizer. However, as Chopin's short narrative unfolds, Edna finds that the forces of conformity and convention are stronger than she believed and that the kind of self-fulfilment she seeks is beyond her. Because of its sympathetic portrait of Edna Pontellier and her refusal to accept the roles that society demands of her, *The Awakening* was a highly controversial book when first published and most of its first reviews were scathingly condemnatory. Allowed to slip out of print after Chopin's death, it remained a forgotten novel for many decades until rediscovered by a new generation. Today it is rightly seen as a classic work of feminist fiction, the tragic portrait of a woman whose desire to escape the constraints imposed on her leads to her destruction.

🎞 **Film version:** *Grand Isle* (1991)

📖 **Read on**
Bayou Folk (short stories)
Charlotte Perkins Gilman, *The Yellow Wallpaper*; Sarah Grand, *The Beth Book*

WILKIE COLLINS (1824–89) UK

THE WOMAN IN WHITE (1860)

In England in the 1860s, a new genre of fiction emerged which became known as 'sensation fiction'. With its antecedents in the Gothic and 'Newgate' novels of earlier decades, 'sensation fiction' peered beneath the surface gentility of Victorian domesticity and revealed a world of bigamy, madness, murder and violence supposedly lurking there. It was all too much for some critics. One described the genre as 'unspeakably disgusting' and castigated its 'ravenous appetite for carrion'. The best-known purveyor of 'sensation fiction' was Wilkie Collins. Collins was the son of a well-known landscape painter and his first literary work was a life of his father but, encouraged by his friend ›› Charles Dickens, he began publishing fiction in the 1850s. *The Woman in White*, published in 1860, is a melodramatic and complicated tale of a conspiracy to dispossess an heiress of her money, filled with dark secrets of lunacy, illegitimacy and mistaken identities and made memorable by the suave and sinister Italian, Count Fosco. The novel unfolds through a series of first person narratives by different characters. Drawing master Walter Hartright tells of his eerie night-time encounter with the eponymous 'woman in white' and of his experiences at Limmeridge House in Cumberland where he meets and falls in love with Laura Fairlie, a girl who bears a striking resemblance to her. Marian Halcombe, Laura's intelligent and strong-minded half-sister, provides further parts of the story in extracts from her diary. Gradually the plot by the villainous Sir Percival Glyde and his accomplice Fosco to gain control of Laura's fortune is revealed. Much of Collins's later fiction is marred by his determination to move away from mystery and suspense, at which he excelled, to fiction with a social purpose, at which he did not, but, in *The Woman in White*, he created the archetypal example of 'sensation fiction'.

🎞 **Film versions:** *The Woman in White* (1948); *The Woman in White* (1997, TV)

📖 **Read on**
The Moonstone
Mary Elizabeth Braddon, *Lady Audley's Secret*; ›› Charles Dickens, *The Mystery of Edwin Drood*; Sheridan Le Fanu, *Uncle Silas*; Bulwer Lytton, *Eugene Aram* (a typical example of the 'Newgate' fiction that flourished in the generation before Collins)

JOSEPH CONRAD (1857–1924) Poland/UK

NOSTROMO (1904)
Few English novelists have created their fiction from the raw material of a life as adventurous as that of Joseph Conrad. He was born Konrad Korzeniowski to Polish parents living in what is now the Ukraine. Both his father and mother were fiercely opposed to Russian domination of their country and suffered exile for their beliefs. Both died before

Conrad reached his teens and he was then brought up by an uncle. In 1876, Conrad began a twenty-year career as a seaman, during which he ran guns for Spanish revolutionaries, sailed on wool clippers to Australia and came to know the ports and cities of the Far East intimately. His experiences at sea were to be transmuted into the novels like *Almayer's Folly*, *Lord Jim* and *The Nigger of the Narcissus* which made his reputation. *Nostromo* is set in a fictional South American republic, Costaguana, where a military insurgency threatens the precarious government currently in power. Charles Gould, English owner of the country's largest silver mines, is acutely aware that his reserves of silver are a prize the competing parties long to seize and he is determined that neither should do so. Two men – the cynical journalist Martin Decoud and the book's anti-hero, Nostromo – are entrusted with the task of hiding the silver from the revolutionaries. Eventually they find a hiding place on an otherwise deserted island off the coast. As Conrad's complex narrative unfolds, Decoud is destroyed by his own cynicism and lack of inner faith while the vainglorious Nostromo, seduced by his own sense of himself as a heroic man of the people and believing that Gould has used and exploited him, is slowly driven further and further into a life of deceit and disenchantment. Only the material power of Gould and his mines survives. As an examination of how men and would-be nations are shaped by social and economic forces beyond their control, *Nostromo* has a sophistication and an intensity unmatched in 20th-century literature.

◄ **Film version:** *Nostromo* (1997, TV)

≋ Read on

Lord Jim; *Typhoon*

B. Traven, *The Treasure of the Sierra Madre*

THE SECRET AGENT (1907)

The Secret Agent is set among the political refugees and anarchist conspirators who gathered in late Victorian London. The central character, Verloc, is an *agent provocateur* in the pay of the Russian embassy, whose seedy Soho shop acts as a meeting place for dissidents from around the world who have washed up in London. Not only is Verloc working with the Russians, he is also passing on information to a Scotland Yard inspector, but his cosy relationship with the authorities is doomed to come to an end. Instructed by his employers at the embassy to manufacture an outrage that will both discredit the anarchists in the city and shock the powers that be into taking a stronger line with them, Verloc decides upon a bomb attack on the Royal Observatory in Greenwich and he dupes his simple-minded brother-in-law Stevie into carrying the explosive. When the bomb explodes prematurely and Stevie dies, Verloc's long-suffering wife Winnie finally turns against him. Her hopes of escape with Comrade Ossipon, one of the habitués of her husband's backroom meetings, are as doomed to disaster as Verloc's inept plots. Taking the basic outline of his story from a real-life attempt to blow up the Royal Observatory in 1894, which ended in the death of the would-be bomber, Conrad creates a claustrophobic world of violence and paranoia that, despite the date of the book's publication, still seems entirely modern. Minor characters, like the walking bomb who calls himself 'the Professor' (he has explosives permanently strapped around his body so that he can blow himself up at any second), are not only memorable but, in the present day, painfully prescient. Conrad's narrative, which invests the basic melodrama of what he calls in his subtitle 'a simple tale' with a cruel and clear-eyed irony, depicts a London anarchist underworld in which every character is morally compromised.

Film versions: *Sabotage* (directed by Alfred Hitchcock, 1936); *The Secret Agent* (with Bob Hoskins as Verloc, 1996)

Read on
Heart of Darkness
John Le Carré, *A Perfect Spy*

STEPHEN CRANE (1871–1900) USA

THE RED BADGE OF COURAGE (1895)
During his short life Stephen Crane gained a reputation as one of the finest journalists of his day and a writer of fiction which was highly admired by such fellow authors as ›› Henry James and ›› Joseph Conrad. His first novel, *Maggie: A Girl of the Streets*, was a pioneering work of American naturalism, set in New York's Bowery slums, while compelling short stories like 'The Open Boat' drew on his journalistic experiences

around the world. However, the work which made his reputation and which remains his finest was the short novel, set in the American Civil War, entitled *The Red Badge of Courage*. The book focuses on Henry Fleming, a young soldier in the Union Army, who dreams of military glory but finds the reality very different from his dreams. His regiment's first encounter with the enemy ends in a mass, panicky retreat and Henry is wounded when he attempts to reason with one of the deserters. In his second experience of battle he is so traumatized by fear that he himself turns and flees. No one notices that he is gone and he wanders aimlessly behind the front lines, witnessing the chaos and confusion of warfare and being moved to anger and despair by the misery he sees epitomized in the death of one ragged soldier. Returning to his regiment, Henry is welcomed back. His cowardice has gone unseen and, in the fighting next day, he appears a model of military courage, picking up and carrying the regimental colours when their original bearer is shot. He even has his 'red badge of courage', the wound of one who has fought, although he knows that he received it in less than heroic circumstances. And, deep in his heart, haunted by the images of death and destruction he has seen, Henry knows that the hero of today can just as easily be the coward of tomorrow.

 Film version: *The Red Badge of Courage* (directed by John Huston, Audie Murphy as Henry, 1951)

 Read on
Maggie: A Girl of the Streets; *The Open Boat and Other Stories*
Erich Maria Remarque, *All Quiet on the Western Front* (another war but the same emotions among the young soldiers)

READ**ON**A**THEME**: MEN AT WAR

Richard Aldington, *Death of a Hero*
Henri Barbusse, *Under Fire*
John Dos Passos, *Three Soldiers*
Norman Mailer, *The Naked and the Dead*
R.H. Mottram, *The Spanish Farm Trilogy*
Siegfried Sassoon, *Memoirs of an Infantry Officer*
Dalton Trumbo, *Johnny Got His Gun*
Gore Vidal, *Williwaw*
Rebecca West, *The Return of the Soldier*
Arnold Zweig, *The Case of Sergeant Grischa*

DANIEL DEFOE (1660–1731) UK

ROBINSON CRUSOE (1719)

Born into a Nonconformist family named Foe (he did not add the extra letters to his name until he was in his early forties), Daniel Defoe led an extraordinarily chequered career. At various times in his life, he was a hosiery merchant in London, a participant in the Monmouth Rebellion, the owner of a tile factory in Tilbury and an undercover agent for the government in the north of England and Scotland. He was also an exceptionally prolific, pioneer journalist, producing hundreds of polemical pamphlets and newspaper articles, most of them anonymously. He did not begin writing fiction until he was approaching sixty. Defoe's imagination was stirred by the story of the real-life sailor Alexander Selkirk, who was marooned on a desert island in 1704, and he began to write what became *Robinson Crusoe*. What fascinated Defoe about Selkirk's experience was the idea of a civilized man forced to confront the natural world stripped of all that made him civilized. How would such a man cope with the challenges? Crusoe, when he is shipwrecked on his island, has little but his resourcefulness and his ingenuity to sustain him. None the less he succeeds in adapting himself to the alien environment and, as he records in the journal he keeps during his long endurance test, he survives there for nearly 30 years. Probably the most famous scenes in the book record Crusoe's alarming discovery of strange footprints in the sand on his island home and his subsequent encounter with Man Friday, the native he rescues from the cannibals who use the island as a venue for their grisly feasts. Combining the exotic fascination of the kind of travel literature that was growing in popularity at the time it was written with the kind of inner voyage described in spiritual autobiographies, *Robinson Crusoe* has retained its fame and popularity for nearly three centuries.

📽 **Film version:** *Robinson Crusoe* (directed by Luis Buñuel, 1954)

📚 **Read on**
Moll Flanders; *Roxana*
R.M. Ballantyne, *Coral Island* (three youths demonstrate all the manly,

Victorian virtues when they are shipwrecked on a desert island); J.M. Coetzee, *Foe*; William Golding, *Lord of the Flies*

CHARLES DICKENS (1812–70) UK

BLEAK HOUSE (1853)

Opening with a brilliantly sustained description of London swathed in impenetrable mists, Dickens leads readers from the literal fog that enshrouds the city to the metaphorical fog that lies at the heart of the Chancery legal system and at the heart of the case of Jarndyce v. Jarndyce in which nearly all the characters in the novel are enmeshed. Esther Summerson, narrator of parts of the book, is a supposed orphan who, together with the young wards of court, Richard Carstone and Ada Clare, comes to live with John Jarndyce at his home, Bleak House. Jarndyce is a good and honourable man and he has turned his back on the endless law case which carries his name, aware that it blights the lives of all those who come into contact with it. As he grows up, Richard Carstone is unable to accept his guardian's wisdom in steering clear of Jarndyce v. Jarndyce. In love with his fellow ward of court, Ada, he sees the case as his road to fortune. Soon he is dragged into a soul-destroying obsession with it. Meanwhile, Esther's quiet virtues attract the love of both her guardian and the surgeon Allan Woodcourt. Around this central story of the wards in court circles Dickens's usual rich panoply of characters, from Jo the crossing sweeper to Sir Leicester Dedlock, proud and pompous representative of an ancient landed family, and his wife, haunted by a past she cannot acknowledge, from Krook, the shabby, drunken shopkeeper who meets the grisliest of ends, to Tulkinghorn, the sinister lawyer intent on learning the truth about Lady Dedlock. All, whether they know it or not, are caught up in the hypocrisy and inhumanity that the Court of Chancery represents. With its superbly worked out structure and interlocking narratives, *Bleak House* is the most compelling of all Dickens's indictments of a society indifferent to the suffering in its midst.

⮒ Read on

Little Dorrit; *Our Mutual Friend*
➤➤ Anthony Trollope, *The Way We Live Now*

GREAT EXPECTATIONS (1861)

Philip Pirrip, better known to himself and others as 'Pip', is a young orphan living on the Kentish marshes with his formidable and much older sister and her good-hearted but unsophisticated husband, the blacksmith Joe Gargery. On one memorable day he is suddenly confronted, in the local churchyard, by the escaped convict, Abel Magwitch. Frightened of Magwitch and yet pitying him, Pip brings him food but the convict is soon recaptured and returned to the hulks to await transportation to Australia. Pip's encounter with him fades in his memory. Summoned to the house of the eccentric Miss Havisham, a recluse since she was jilted on her wedding day, he meets her ward, the beautiful Estella, and loses his heart to her. Estella meets all his boyish protestations of love with disdain but he continues to worship her as he grows up. As a young man, he is suddenly taken away from the world he knows when he is informed by the lawyer Jaggers that he has 'great expectations' and that a mysterious benefactor is prepared to subsidize his transformation into a gentleman. Travelling to London, Pip joins forces with his room-mate, the amiable Herbert Pocket, acquires the superficial polish needed to accompany his rise in status and establishes himself as a young man about town. He always assumes that his hidden well-wisher is Miss Havisham and that he can, therefore, continue to hope for the love of Estella. But the illegal return of Magwitch from the penal colony reveals how mistaken he has been in all his assumptions. *Great Expectations* is peopled, as Dickens's novels always are, by comic eccentrics and grotesques but, at its heart, it is the narrative of one young man's progress towards a deeper understanding of himself and of the true personal history which has shaped his character.

Film version: *Great Expectations* (directed by David Lean, John Mills as Pip, 1946)

Read on
David Copperfield; *Nicholas Nickleby*
W. Somerset Maugham, *Of Human Bondage*

READONATHEME: ORPHANS

(and the hard times they sometimes have)
- ›› Charlotte Brontë, *Jane Eyre*
- ›› Charles Dickens, *Oliver Twist*
  - Frances Hodgson Burnett, *The Secret Garden*
- ›› Rudyard Kipling, *Kim*
  - L.M. Montgomery, *Anne of Green Gables*
  - Johanna Spyri, *Heidi*
- ›› Mark Twain, *The Adventures of Tom Sawyer*

BENJAMIN DISRAELI (1804–81) UK

SYBIL (1845)

Although he is remembered today as a politician, Disraeli came from a literary family (his father Isaac d'Israeli was the author of six volumes entitled *Curiosities of Literature*) and his first fame came as a writer. He published *Vivian Grey* when he was still only in his early twenties and this witty society novel was followed by several others. He once told a friend, tongue only partially in cheek, that, 'When I want to read a novel, I write one', and even as his political career began to take off in the 1840s, he continued to publish fiction. *Sybil* was a deliberate attempt to address the state of the nation in a novel. Its alternative title was 'The Two Nations' and Disraeli's aim was to show that English society was indeed divided into two nations, the rich and the poor, between whom, as a character in the novel says, 'there is no intercourse and no sympathy; who are as ignorant of each other's habits, thoughts, and feelings, as if they were dwellers in different zones, or inhabitants of different planets; who are formed by a different breeding, are fed by a different food, are ordered by different manners, and are not governed by the same laws'. The eponymous heroine is the young daughter of a Chartist worker, Walter Gerard, who, together with the journalist Stephen Morley, represents what Disraeli sees as the best in the working classes. Morley and Gerard, with their moral seriousness and urge to improve their own lives and the lot of others, are contrasted with the idle selfishness of the aristocracy. Symbolic reconciliation between the two halves of the nation comes with the marriage of Sybil and Egremont, an aristocrat who has come to acknowledge the irresponsibility of his own class. Disraeli's view of working-class life is marred by a paternalistic sentimentality but there is no doubting his genuine sympathy with the sufferings of the new workers the Industrial Revolution had created.

🕮 Read on

Coningsby

>> Charles Dickens, *Hard Times*; >> George Eliot, *Felix Holt*; >> Elizabeth Gaskell, *North and South*; Charles Kingsley, *Alton Locke*; >> Anthony Trollope, *The Prime Minister*

ALFRED DÖBLIN (1878–1957) Germany

BERLIN ALEXANDERPLATZ (1929)

Every major European city has its own modernist masterpiece. Dublin, of course, has ›› Joyce's *Ulysses*. Paris has ›› Proust, St Petersburg Andrei Bely's extraordinary novel simply entitled *Petersburg*. Berlin has a remarkable and impressive book published in the difficult days of the Weimar Republic, on the eve of the Nazi rise to power: Alfred Döblin's *Berlin Alexanderplatz*. The novel focuses on a small-time crook named Franz Biberkopf as he is released from prison. Biberkopf, who has a violent past, is intent on living a reformed and decent life but, returning to his old haunts in the Alexanderplatz area of Berlin, he finds it impossible to escape a world of prostitutes, petty thievery, thuggery and the emerging street violence of the times. Using interior monologue, Berlin slang, psychological insight drawn from his early academic training and cinematic techniques of jump-cutting and visual metaphor adapted for literary purposes, Döblin creates a rich portrait of Biberkopf and the Berlin he inhabits. As an evocation of the sprawling anonymity and dangerous maelstrom of the modern city, *Berlin Alexanderplatz* remains a remarkable achievement. It was influenced by Döblin's reading of Joyce (although he later became irritated by endless comparisons of his novel with Joyce's, Döblin admitted that 'his work was wind for my sails'). Döblin was a Berliner by birth and studied medicine and psychiatry before turning to literature. During the Nazi years he fled Germany (he was Jewish) and lived in France and then America, where he was an unlikely recipient of MGM's munificence, living in Los Angeles and earning money as a scriptwriter. He returned to Europe after the war and died in 1957. Döblin wrote other novels which grappled with themes of alienation and despair in contemporary life but none matched the experimental brilliance of *Berlin Alexanderplatz*.

🎬 **Film version:** *Berlin Alexanderplatz* (multi-part series directed by Rainer Werner Fassbinder, 1980, TV)

📖 **Read on**
Andrei Bely, *Petersburg*; Christopher Isherwood, *Goodbye to Berlin*; Robert Musil, *The Man Without Qualities*

FYODOR DOSTOEVSKY (1821–81) Russia

CRIME AND PUNISHMENT (1866)

The psychological intensity and raw power of Dostoevsky's fiction emerged from the dramatic events of his own life. As a young man he was arrested and tried for revolutionary activity and sentenced to death. He even faced a firing squad in a mock execution before he was told his sentence had been reduced to hard labour and he was sent to a Siberian prison camp. On his release from prison, he was a changed man, a convert to more conservative political views and to a new religious faith which was to be tested in the years to come by the deaths in swift succession of his wife and his much-loved elder brother. His three great novels are *Crime and Punishment*, *The Idiot* and *The Brothers Karamazov*. Of these, the earliest is *Crime and Punishment*, the story of Raskolnikov, a young and impoverished student, who is convinced he is such an extraordinary man that he is not bound by conventional morality. He decides to prove his special status by committing murder and chooses as his victim the elderly money-lender, Alyona Ivanovna. Taking on himself the role of judge and jury that he believes is his prerogative, as a member of the intellectual and moral elite, he comes to the conclusion that she is a parasite and unworthy to live. Entering her rooms he kills both the pawnbroker and her sister who disturbs him while he is looking for money. After the killings, Raskolnikov discovers that he is not quite the superman he believed he was. Enslaved by his own feelings of guilt and remorse, he falls prey to a paranoia and misery that can only be ended by confession to his crime. Dostoevsky's novel records the slow disintegration of Raskolnikov's personality and his painful journey towards some kind of ambivalent redemption.

☙ Read on

Notes From the Underground
➤➤ Albert Camus, *The Fall*, ➤➤ Joseph Conrad, *Under Western Eyes*, ➤➤ Leo Tolstoy, *Resurrection*

THE BROTHERS KARAMAZOV (1880)

Fyodor Karamazov is a rich and dissolute man who has fathered three legitimate sons in two marriages and is rumoured also to be the father of Smerdyakov, the mean-spirited and malicious epileptic who works as a servant in the Karamazov household.

Each of the brothers represents a different way of approaching life and its meaning (or lack of it). The eldest, Dmitri, is a sensualist like his father, interested only in the pleasures of the flesh. Ivan is a rationalist and atheist, unable to reconcile the idea of a supreme being with the suffering he sees in the world, who seems to be permanently angry with the God in whom he doesn't believe. Alyosha is a kind and gentle man, as fervent in his Christian beliefs as Ivan is in his atheism, who is attached to a monastery where he studies at the feet of a saintly elder named Zosima. In the course of the novel, Dmitri and his father come into conflict, both over money and over a beautiful young woman named Grushenka. The two men come to blows and Dmitri is heard to threaten his father so, when Fyodor is found dead, suspicion falls on his eldest son and he is brought to trial. The truth about Fyodor's murder, which never fully emerges, is that he was killed by Smerdyakov, who has listened to Ivan's tirades against God and come to believe that there is no right and no wrong in the world. In death, as in life, the brutal Fyodor exercises his power over all his sons and only Alyosha, with his belief in the power of love to conquer suffering, survives undamaged. Dostoevsky's enormously ambitious novel grapples with the most profound questions of good and evil and the meaning of life, while remaining a darkly gripping saga of one family's disintegration and near-destruction.

◄ **Film versions:** *The Brothers Karamazov* (1958); *The Brothers Karamazov* (Russian version, 1969)

≋ **Read on**
The Gambler; The Idiot

ALEXANDRE DUMAS (1802–70) France

THE COUNT OF MONTE CRISTO

Dumas was the most successful French novelist of his day and his historical adventures, which continue to be widely read, have been the basis for dozens of plays, films and TV series over the years. His most famous books are those which feature the Three Musketeers (Athos, Porthos and Aramis) and their Gascon friend D'Artagnan in breathtaking sword fights and swashbuckling exploits in 17th-century France. However, his best novel may well be *The Count of Monte Cristo*, both high adventure and a penetrating study of justice and vengeance. The book opens as the hero Edmond Dantès returns to Marseille from a sea voyage. Life seems good. He is about to win promotion to ship's captain and he is set to marry the beautiful Mercédès – but Dantès does not realize that he has enemies plotting his downfall. Seizing the opportunity offered by Dantès's naïve willingness to deliver a package to an exiled Napoleonic marshal and thus embroil himself unwittingly in political intrigue, Danglars, who envies the young man's promotion, and Fernand, who lusts after Mercédès, join forces to finger him as a Bonapartist agent. Villefort, the magistrate before whom Dantès is brought, has his own reasons for silencing the young man and he is condemned to perpetual imprisonment in the infamous Chateau d'If. The years pass and Dantès's only companion is the Abbé Faria, an old man long incarcerated for his political beliefs. Faria tells Edmond of a great treasure hidden on the island of Monte Cristo and, when the old priest dies, Dantès, with the ingenuity born of despair, escapes by sewing himself into the dead man's shroud which is cast into the sea. He retrieves the treasure from the island and, now one of the wealthiest and most powerful men in France, he is free to pursue his revenge.

📖 **Film versions:** *The Count of Monte Cristo* (with Robert Donat, 1934); *The Count of Monte Cristo* (with Richard Chamberlain, 1975, TV)

📖 **Read on**
The Three Musketeers; *The Queen's Necklace*
Baroness Orczy, *The Scarlet Pimpernel*; Rafael Sabatini, *Captain Blood* (two further swashbucklers in the tradition Dumas established)

READ**ON**A**THEME**: SWASH AND BUCKLE

Sir Arthur Conan Doyle, *The Exploits of Brigadier Gerard*
>> Alexandre Dumas, *Twenty Years After* (the ageing Musketeers assemble for one last hurrah)
J. Meade Falkner, *Moonfleet*
>> H. Rider Haggard, *Montezuma's Daughter*
Anthony Hope, *The Prisoner of Zenda*
Rafael Sabatini, *Scaramouche*
>> Robert Louis Stevenson, *Treasure Island*
P.C. Wren, *Beau Geste*

GEORGE ELIOT (1819–80) UK

ADAM BEDE (1859)

Born in Warwickshire and the recipient of a much broader education than was usual for a woman in the first half of the 19th century, Mary Anne (or Marian) Evans began her literary career by making use of her knowledge of European languages and working as a translator. Her first fiction, *Scenes of Clerical Life*, appeared under George Eliot, the male pseudonym she had adopted in 1857. >> Dickens was one of the few people perceptive enough to recognize that the stories were the work of a woman, writing that, if the book were not the work of a woman, 'then should I begin to believe that I am a woman myself'. *Adam Bede* followed two years later. The eponymous central character is a carpenter in a small village in the Midlands who is in love with the vain and flirtatious Hetty Sorrel, the niece of a local farmer. Hetty, dreaming of social advancement, responds to the interest shown in her by the local squire, Arthur Donnithorne, as Adam looks on with ill-concealed concern. Adam is proved right in his anxieties about Hetty, who is first seduced and then abandoned by Donnithorne. Hetty now agrees to marry Adam but she is not only still distressed by her earlier lover's faithlessness, she is also pregnant and, before the wedding can take place, she disappears. Hetty's flighty flirtatiousness, eventually punished by her arrest and trial for the supposed murder of her child, is contrasted with the steady moral virtue of the Methodist preacher, Dinah Morris, who provides comfort in their troubles for both Adam and Hetty. George Eliot's first full-length novel, inspired by an account her aunt gave her of spending the night with a young woman condemned to die for infanticide, is a major work of Victorian realism, an example of her belief that the lives of the poor and the obscure deserved the attention of novelists as much as those of the rich and powerful.

🕮 Read on

The Mill on the Floss; *Scenes of Clerical Life*
>> Thomas Hardy, *Tess of the D'Urbervilles*

MIDDLEMARCH (1871–2)

Described by ›› Virginia Woolf as 'one of the few English novels for grown-up people', *Middlemarch* is set in the provincial town that gives the book its title, in the years running up to the Great Reform Act of 1832. At the heart of Eliot's panorama of English small-town life are the stories of two people who long to break free from the constraints it imposes on them. One is Dorothea Brooke, whose idealistic visions of wedded life as intellectual partnership are destroyed by the reality of marriage to the desiccated and pedantic scholar Casaubon. Her dreams of collaboration in a work of world-shaking scholarly brilliance come to nothing as she realizes that Casaubon's never-to-be-finished 'Key to All Mythologies' is, like its author, deeply flawed and inadequate. The other is the doctor Tertius Lydgate, struggling to introduce new medical ideas to a provincial society deeply suspicious of change, who makes a disastrous match with Rosamund Vincy, a beautiful but brainless social climber. Around the lives of Dorothea and Lydgate, Eliot constructs a monumental portrait of everyday life, peopled by dozens of compelling characters, from the wealthy banker Bulstrode, desperate to hide the shady secrets of his past, to Will Ladislaw, Casaubon's young cousin whom Dorothea loves and for whom she forfeits an inheritance when her first husband dies. *Middlemarch* is an extraordinarily rich and rewarding novel but, like so much of Eliot's fiction, it is fundamentally a tribute to the value and worth of ordinary, unsung lives – a recognition that, in the final words of the book, 'the growing good of the world is partly dependent on unhistoric acts; and that things are not so ill with you and me as they might have been, is half owing to the number who lived faithfully a hidden life, and rest in unvisited tombs.'

⮞ Read on

Daniel Deronda; *Felix Holt, the Radical*

›› Elizabeth Gaskell, *Wives and Daughters*; Winifred Holtby, *South Riding*

WILLIAM FAULKNER (1897–1962) USA

THE SOUND AND THE FURY (1929)

Throughout his fiction, William Faulkner was concerned to record what he saw as the moral degeneracy of the American Deep South and the dying post-Civil War culture into which he had himself been born. Probably his greatest single achievement was *The Sound and the Fury*, a complex and ambitious novel which takes its title from Macbeth's description of life in the Shakespeare play ('a tale told by an idiot, full of sound and fury') and which has a first section that is indeed a tale told by an 'idiot', the severely retarded Benjy Compson. Set in Faulkner's fictional Yoknapatawpha County, the book reveals the story of the Compson family in three further sections, two told by Benjy's brothers and a final one seen from the viewpoint of their negro servants. At the heart of the story is Caddy Compson. To Benjy, Caddy is his beloved sister whose name echoes forever in his limited mind. To Quentin, narrator of the second section (set eighteen years earlier than the others), she is the object of a guilty incestuous obsession which eventually drives him to take his own life. To Jason, the bitter and twisted narrator of the third section, she is the cause of all his troubles in life. As the interlocking narratives unfold, readers witness the disintegration of the Compson family in a welter of alcohol, mutual hatreds, greed and despair. Faulkner made much use in his fiction of modernist techniques (stream of consciousness, multiple and unreliable narrators) pioneered by European writers such as ›› Virginia Woolf and ›› James Joyce. However, he combined these with a particularly American tradition of writing about the Deep South to produce novels which chart moral decline with merciless precision. *The Sound and the Fury*, in many ways his finest work, has all the cruel inevitability and emotional power of a Greek tragedy.

◄ Film version: *The Sound and the Fury* (1959)

➳ Read on
Absalom! Absalom!; *Intruder in the Dust*; *Light in August*
Harper Lee, *To Kill a Mockingbird*; Carson McCullers, *The Ballad of the Sad Café*; Flannery O'Connor, *Wise Blood*; Eudora Welty, *Delta Wedding* (all for very different views of the American South)

HENRY FIELDING (1707–54) UK

TOM JONES (1749)

Fielding only turned to the novel when the stage was effectively closed to him. Over a nine-year period the young Fielding wrote more than twenty plays but his career as a satirical dramatist, lampooning the corruption and hypocrisies of Sir Robert Walpole's government in plays like *Tom Thumb* and *The Historical Register for the Year 1736* came to an end when the targets of his genial venom introduced the Licensing Act of 1737, bringing the stage under a stricter censorship. Beginning with parodic variations on Samuel Richardson's lengthy, moralistic fiction (*Shamela* and *Joseph Andrews*), Fielding soon became a master novelist. His finest achievement was *Tom Jones*, the picaresque saga of an amiable but fallible young man at large in a world of temptation and trouble. Tom is a foundling, brought up by the benevolent Mr Allworthy at his country home. Tom's great enemy in life is the malicious Blifil, Allworthy's nephew and heir, who schemes to have his rival disgraced and expelled from the family home. His great love, despite his affairs with a gamekeeper's daughter and with a promiscuous aristocrat, is Sophia Western, who has long been promised in marriage to Blifil but who hates the prospect of giving him her hand and eventually flees home to avoid doing so. The novel charts Tom's and Sophia's roundabout journey, beset by the machinations of Blifil and others, towards eventual happiness and marriage. Not everybody was impressed by *Tom Jones* when it was first published. 'I am shocked to hear you quote from so vicious a novel,' Dr Johnson said to a friend and there were some who attributed the two earthquake shocks that hit

London in 1749 to the malign influence of Fielding's book. However, it has long survived Johnson's strictures to become one of the best-loved and most influential of all English novels.

🎞 **Film version:** *Tom Jones* (directed by Tony Richardson, starring Albert Finney as Tom, 1963)

📖 **Read on**
Joseph Andrews
Tobias Smollett, *The Adventures of Roderick Random*

F. SCOTT FITZGERALD (1896–1940) USA

THE GREAT GATSBY (1925)
Some novelists define the age in which they write and few writers did so more effectively than F. Scott Fitzgerald. He coined the term 'Jazz Age' for the era of febrile pleasure-seeking that followed the First World War and he provided its most characteristic fiction in his finest novel, *The Great Gatsby*. The short narrative focuses on the enigmatic, fabulously wealthy Jay Gatsby who throws wild and legendary parties while yearning for the elusive Daisy Buchanan, once his lover and now married to someone else. Rumours about Gatsby and the source of his wealth abound. Perhaps he was a German spy during the War. Possibly

he once murdered a man. More convincingly, he is said to have connections with bootleggers and gangsters. Narrator Nick Carraway, Daisy's cousin, is the man who observes Gatsby's downfall. Renting a property next to Gatsby's mansion, venue for the glamorous parties, he befriends him, intrigued by the mystery that surrounds him. Gatsby persuades Nick to reintroduce him to Daisy and the two resume their affair. Tom Buchanan, Daisy's husband, is himself involved in an adulterous relationship with another woman but he is infuriated by his wife's infidelity when he discovers it. Gatsby struggles to convince Daisy that she should leave Tom; Tom threatens to reveal the secrets of Gatsby's past. The scene is set for the novel's culmination and the tragedies to unfold. *The Great Gatsby* is a poetic and moving study of a man who comes from nowhere to achieve everything (wealth, social status, glamour) that America promises its citizens but is obliged eventually to recognize the hollowness at the heart of the promise. No book has ever caught more perfectly and precisely the power of the American Dream and the pain of the disillusionment that follows the realization that it is ultimately unattainable.

🎬 **Film versions:** *The Great Gatsby* (with Alan Ladd as Gatsby, 1949); *The Great Gatsby* (with Robert Redford as Gatsby, 1974)

📖 **Read on**
The Beautiful and the Damned; *Tender is the Night*
▶▶ Ernest Hemingway, *The Sun Also Rises*; Anita Loos, *Gentlemen Prefer Blondes* (a farcical rather than melancholic portrait of the Jazz Age); Dawn Powell, *A Time to be Born*

GUSTAVE FLAUBERT (1821–80) France

MADAME BOVARY (1857)

Gustave Flaubert wrote a number of very different novels in his career, ranging from the sensuous and exotic historical narrative *Salammbô*, set in ancient Carthage, to *Sentimental Education*, an ironic *Bildungsroman*, but it is the domestic tragedy of *Madame Bovary* for which he is best remembered. Attacked for its supposed obscenity when it first appeared and the subject of a public prosecution, the story of the bored and frustrated doctor's wife, Emma Bovary, is one of the great novels of the 19th century. Charles Bovary is a dull and mediocre man, a doctor with a practice in a small French town, who marries the young and unworldly Emma. As Flaubert's cruelly perceptive and ironic account of the Bovary marriage unfolds, Emma, weary of the everyday tedium of provincial life, excites herself by playing with the idea of an affair with a similarly romantic law clerk named Léon and is eventually seduced by the wealthy womanizer, Rodolphe. Despite the growing scandal that his wife is attracting in the small and small-minded community in which they live, Bovary remains oblivious to his wife's infidelity. His own professional reputation is ruined by a botched operation on a club foot. Meanwhile Emma, cast off by Rodolphe, plunges into debt and into a renewed relationship, this time sexual, with Léon. Her indiscretions, both emotional and financial, inevitably catch up with her and, despite her increasingly frenzied attempts to escape the consequences of her actions, she is doomed. Emma is a dreamer, seduced by romantic notions of life and love which everyday reality cannot possibly match. Her love affairs, rather than being grand passions, are tawdry and, seen with the cold eye that Flaubert provides, even slightly ridiculous. In Flaubert's uncompromising tragedy of ordinary life, it is the discrepancy between dream and reality that finally destroys her.

◤ **Film version:** *Madame Bovary* (1949); *Madame Bovary* (directed by Claude Chabrol, with Isabelle Huppert as Emma, 1991)

⮱ **Read on**
Sentimental Education
>> Leo Tolstoy, *Anna Karenina*

THEODORE FONTANE (1819–98) Germany

EFFI BRIEST (1895)

For the first few decades of his career, Fontane was known primarily as a poet and travel writer (he published a number of books about his experiences in mid-19th-century England) but he began to publish fiction in his fifties and is now recognized as the first and greatest master of the German realistic novel. *Effi Briest*, which appeared only a few years before Fontane's death, is his finest work. The central character, reminiscent of >> Flaubert's Emma Bovary, is a beautiful young woman married to an older man. Effi Briest is only seventeen when she is married off to Baron Geert von Innstetten, a civil servant twice her age. The match, although considered socially suitable, is a disastrous one. Innstetten takes his new bride to a small town on the Baltic coast but his work takes him away for long periods of time and Effi is bored, unhappy and isolated. She becomes perfect prey for the charming but selfish womanizer Crampas and she embarks on a short-lived affair. As the years pass and Innstetten and Effi move to Berlin, her indiscretion looks destined to remain her secret but her husband chances upon old letters between the two lovers and her past returns to ruin her. Innstetten divorces her and society turns its back on her. Husband and former lover fight a duel and Crampas is killed. The rigid morality that governs the lives of all the characters is shown to have destroyed the lives of three of them. Fontane has proved a major influence on German literature in the last century. Thomas Mann declared that *Effi Briest* was 'one of the six most significant novels ever written' and more recent novelists (Heinrich Böll, for one) show the powerful effect of Fontane's vision of destructively inflexible moral codes continuing in very different social circumstances. His novels, and particularly *Effi Briest*, deserve a wider readership outside Germany.

◣ **Film version:** *Effie Briest* (directed by Rainer Werner Fassbinder, 1974)

⮂ Read on
Cecile; *Jenny Treibel*
Heinrich Böll, *The Lost Honour of Katharina Blum*; ›› Gustave Flaubert, *Madame Bovary*; Heinrich von Kleist, *The Marquise von O.*; ›› Émile Zola, *Thérèse Raquin*

FORD MADOX FORD (1873–1939) UK

THE GOOD SOLDIER (1915)

Born Ford Herman Hueffer, the son of Francis Hueffer, music critic for *The Times*, and the grandson of the painter Ford Madox Brown, Ford Madox Ford (who changed his name in 1919 in the wake of post-war anti-German feelings) was brought up in what he called 'the hothouse atmosphere of Pre-Raphaelism, where I was being trained for a genius'. He published volumes of verse, biography and criticism from the 1890s until his death, collaborated with ➤➤ Joseph Conrad on several works of fiction and, as founder and editor of *The English Review* and *Transatlantic Review*, was a major influence on the modern movement in English literature. Of the novels he wrote himself, the one that has best survived the passage of time is *The Good Soldier*. Opening with the remark by the narrator, John Dowell, that, 'This is the saddest story I have ever heard', the book chronicles the failing relationships of two couples. For many years Dowell and his wife Florence travel regularly to a German spa where Florence can take treatment for her supposed heart problems. There they meet and befriend Edward Ashburnham, the 'good soldier' of the title, and his wife Leonora. Ashburnham, weak but charming, is a philanderer, dependent on his wife, who colludes with him in his love affairs. As the intricate structure of Ford's plot unfolds, deception and betrayal are revealed and Ashburnham's obsessive infatuation with his ward Nancy Rufford leads to a multiple tragedy. Ford's other major achievement is the epic four-volume *Parade's End*, published between 1924 and 1928, which charts the life of Christopher Tietjens as he struggles to re-adjust to a post-war world for which his upbringing has failed to prepare him, but *The Good Soldier*, with the unforgiving clarity and ironies of its plot, is his one book that undoubtedly deserves classic status.

🕮 Read on
The Fifth Queen; *Parade's End*
>> Evelyn Waugh, *Brideshead Revisited*

E.M. FORSTER (1879–1970) UK

HOWARDS END (1910)
'In no book', Forster once said in an interview, 'have I got more down than the people I like, the person I think I am, and the people who irritate me.' Despite this modest assessment of his work, Forster remains one of the most admired English novelists of the 20th century and a brilliantly perceptive guide to the kind of emotional reticence and awkwardness so often seen as typically English. His most famous novel is probably *A Passage to India*, a story of the unbridgeable gulf between Indians and English under the Raj, but *Howards End* is arguably his most characteristic and successful work. The novel focuses on the complicated relationship between two families – the cultured and idealistic Schlegels and the more materialistic Wilcoxes. The Schlegel sisters, Margaret and Helen, both respond admiringly to the

apparent practicality of the Wilcoxes, father Henry and two sons, Paul and Charles. Helen is briefly engaged to Paul before she realizes that she cannot go through with the marriage. Later, after a subsequent estrangement between the two families ends, Margaret befriends Mrs Wilcox, the owner of the country house Howards End, symbol of all that is good and enduring in the story. When Mrs Wilcox dies, Margaret ultimately agrees to become Henry's second wife, unaware that he and Charles have conspired to deprive her of Howards End which Mrs Wilcox bequeathed her in a note they have destroyed. Into this tangled web of deceit and ambivalent emotions steps Leonard Bast, a lower middle-class clerk with aspirations to better himself, who has a short and disastrous affair with Helen. The lives of many of the characters (the Schlegel sisters, Henry and Charles Wilcox, Leonard Bast) are changed and blighted by the events of the novel but the house itself, Howards End, survives as the means of finally uniting the different worlds they represent.

Film version: *Howards End* (directed by James Ivory, starring Anthony Hopkins and Vanessa Redgrave, 1992)

Read on

A Passage to India; *A Room With a View*; *Where Angels Fear to Tread* L.P. Hartley, *Eustace and Hilda*; Kazuo Ishiguro, *The Remains of the Day*; ›› Virginia Woolf, *Night and Day*

MILES FRANKLIN (1879–1954) Australia

MY BRILLIANT CAREER (1901)

Written while the author was still a teenager and focusing on an irrepressibly high-spirited teenage heroine, *My Brilliant Career* is quite clearly thinly disguised autobiography as much as fiction. Although Franklin was later annoyed by the literalness with which critics interpreted the book as nothing but her own story, it is difficult to untangle the real woman who wrote the book from the character at its centre. Sybylla Melvyn is a young girl with dreams of a world beyond the confines of her family's farm in the wilds of the Australian outback. She longs to be a writer but, surrounded by a largely unsympathetic household, she can see no way of fulfilling her ambitions. Only when she visits her grandmother's homestead in a less remote part of the country does she glimpse the life she might be able to lead and here she is distracted by the attentions of would-be suitors. One, the wealthy Harry Beecham, offers Sybylla a real alternative to the backwoods exile she most dreads and she is genuinely attracted to him but she is equally determined to maintain the independence she values. Franklin's novel was a great success when it first appeared and she wrote a sequel, *My Career Goes Bung*, soon afterwards. Her publisher, fearful of the way in which she used real people as the bases for her characters, rejected the manuscript and it was not finally published until 1946. Because of both its setting and its characters, *My Brilliant Career* is often acclaimed as one of the first genuinely Australian novels, possessed of an indigenous vitality that owes little to European or American models. It is also an exuberant coming-of-age story and a feminist classic decades ahead of its time, in which, as Carmen Callil has written, Franklin 'created a character who mouths with incredible charm but deadly accuracy the fears, conflicts and torments of every girl, with an understanding usually associated with writers of the 1960s and 70s.'

⚓ Film version: *My Brilliant Career* (1979)

📖 Read on
My Career Goes Bung
Christina Stead, *For Love Alone*; Olive Schreiner, *The Story of an African Farm*

ELIZABETH GASKELL (1810–65) UK

NORTH AND SOUTH (1854)

Brought up in the small Cheshire town of Knutsford, later recreated as 'Cranford' in the short novel of that title, Elizabeth Stevenson married the Unitarian minister William Gaskell when she was in her early twenties and moved with him to the rapidly expanding industrial city of Manchester. Much of her fiction, most notably the aptly titled *North and South*, drew on her knowledge of the industrialized north of England and the cultural divide which separated it from the south. The heroine of *North and South* is Margaret Hale, transplanted from the idyllic surroundings of Helstone in the south to the grim, northern city of Milton-Northern (Manchester in all but name) when her father, a church minister, decides to move. There she finds herself drawn into the conflict between the workers, with whose plight she sympathizes, and the mill owners, as represented by the powerful personality of John Thornton. Matters are only complicated by Thornton's growing feelings for Margaret and by her own dawning realization that, although she dislikes his attitude towards his workers and although she rejects his early proposal of marriage, she loves him. Mrs Gaskell had already created a portrait of Manchester life and tackled themes of industrial strife and unrest in her first novel, *Mary Barton*. In later novels such as *Sylvia's Lovers* and the posthumously published *Wives and Daughters* she produced plots which explored relationships complicated by misunderstandings and the clash between beliefs and desire. *North and South* works so successfully because it combines Elizabeth Gaskell's social concerns and her wish to use fiction to draw attention to poverty and injustice with her interest in the personal trials and tribulations of her central characters. The novel is a triumph both as a social document and as a story of two people struggling to overcome their differences and acknowledge their love.

≋ Read on
Cranford; *Mary Barton*; *Wives and Daughters*
Mrs Linnaeus Banks, *A Manchester Man* (an unjustly neglected novel, first published in the 1870s and set in Manchester in the early years of the Industrial Revolution); ›› Charlotte Brontë, *Shirley*; ›› Charles Dickens, *Hard Times*

STELLA GIBBONS (1902–89) UK

COLD COMFORT FARM (1932)

Cold Comfort Farm tells the story of Flora Poste, a sophisticated young lady, 'possessed of every art and grace save that of earning her own living'. Orphaned at twenty, she concludes that her only option is to go and stay with distant relations, the Starkadders of Cold Comfort Farm, Howling, Sussex. The farm is a far cry from the metropolitan haunts to which Flora is used and its inhabitants very different from the Bright Young Things of her acquaintance. There is the monumentally gloomy Judith Starkadder, convinced of the inevitable disasters to be visited upon the farm and all who live there. There is Seth, her priapic son, forever 'mollocking' with Moll at the mill and Violet at the vicarage; Amos, preaching of 'the reeking red pits of the Lord's eternal wrathy fires' that lie in wait for all; Adam Lambsbreath, the aged farmhand who milks the cows Graceless, Pointless, Feckless and Aimless; and Elfine, the fey creature of nature who wanders the hills with 'only the wild birds and the rabbits and the spying maggies for company'. Brooding over all is the figure of Aunt Ada Doom who once saw 'something nasty in the woodshed' and never allows any member of the family to forget it. A satire of the lugubriously fatalistic fiction of writers like ➤➤ Hardy and Mary Webb, in which tragedy and disaster hang permanently over the rural landscapes of England, *Cold Comfort Farm* has claims to being the funniest English novel of the 20th century. Its author, Stella Gibbons, first gained attention as a poet and *Cold Comfort Farm* was her first novel. She never repeated its success, despite returning to its characters and setting in later books like *Conference at Cold Comfort*

Farm, but the adventures of Flora Poste among the Starkadders live on as a reminder of her unique comic imagination.

🎬 **Film version:** *Cold Comfort Farm* (directed by John Schlesinger, 1995, TV)

📖 **Read on**
The Bachelor; *The Matchmaker*
›› Thomas Hardy, *The Return of the Native*; A.G. Macdonell, *England, Their England*; Mary Webb, *Gone to Earth*

GEORGE GISSING (1857–1903) UK

NEW GRUB STREET (1891)

George Gissing was the most gifted of those English novelists who chose to write in the naturalistic style pioneered by French writers like ›› Zola and ›› Maupassant, and his work shares with them a bitter condemnation of a social order in which poverty and despair are allowed to flourish unchecked. His most famous novel, however, is a painfully accurate portrait, as insightful today as it was in the 1890s, of the vicissitudes and indignities of the literary life. The two central characters of the novel stand at each end of the literary spectrum as Gissing envisages it. Edward Reardon, clearly a version of Gissing himself, is a fine writer but he is hampered by poverty and by marriage to a woman who cannot sympathize with his art. Jasper Milvain is a glib and facile reviewer with his eye firmly set on worldly success. As the novel unfolds, we watch Milvain's inexorable rise and Reardon's equally inevitable downfall. Gissing knew well the poverty and misery of late Victorian London which he evoked so brilliantly in his novels. A classical scholar whose academic career was ruined when he was imprisoned briefly as a young man for theft, he became a prolific novelist but it was only towards the end of his life that he began to earn enough to free him from haunting financial anxieties. Beginning with *Workers in the Dawn* (1880), Gissing wrote nearly twenty works of fiction in his relatively short career, books in which characters struggle against poverty, injustice and the constraints of traditional morality. The typical Gissing hero is a man like Reardon in *New Grub Street*, sensitive and intelligent but condemned to a life in which his gifts are little recognized. With a relish that is almost sadistic (or masochistic, if one considers how much he identified with his central characters), Gissing charts his heroes' decline and eventual fall.

☙ Read on

The Nether World; *The Private Papers of Henry Ryecroft*
▶▶ Thomas Hardy, *Jude the Obscure*; George Moore, *Esther Waters*; Arthur Morrison, *A Child of the Jago*

JOHANN WOLFGANG VON GOETHE
(1749–1832) Germany

THE SORROWS OF YOUNG WERTHER (1774)

One of the first works to announce the arrival of a new spirit of melancholic romanticism in European culture, Goethe's short novel tells the story of the obsessive love of the young artist Werther for the beautiful Lotte who is engaged to another man, Albert. Through a series of letters the doomed progress of Werther's one-sided affair is recorded, culminating in his suicide when he can bear the pain of his unrequited love no longer. *The Sorrows of Young Werther*, written when Goethe was a young man in his twenties, was an astonishingly influential work in the years immediately after its first publication. Young men dressed as Werther, spoke and acted like Werther and even, in some extreme instances, chose to end their lives like Werther. Today the novel may seem stilted and lacking in conviction at times but it remains worth reading if only to learn the source of so many of the ideas about romantic love that permeated the late 18th and early 19th centuries and that still have the power to move us today. In the course of his long life, Goethe became the most important figure in the history of German literature and a philosopher and polymath with interests ranging from the theory of colours to human anatomy. His most famous literary work is the epic drama *Faust*, with its story of a man prepared to sell his soul to the devil in return for knowledge and power, and he also wrote a number of other novels in addition to *The Sorrows of Young Werther*. (*Elective Affinities*, for example, is a cool, even heartless, examination of marriage, featuring a couple who are drawn into relationships with another man and woman.) However, it was his first novel that proved most influential in its day and that continues to attract readers in the present.

⮞ Read on
Elective Affinities
Benjamin Constant, *Adolphe*; ➤➤ Hermann Hesse, *Gertrud*

NIKOLAI GOGOL (1809–52) Russia

DEAD SOULS (1842)
Con-man Chichikov travels through the country, buying from their masters the 'dead souls' of serfs who have passed away in the real world but are officially still alive until the next census. Since, in 19th-century Russia, wealth is measured by the number of serfs as much as by the amount of land an individual owns, Chichikov is soon, in theory, one of the richest men in the country. Around this farcical story, Gogol constructs a wide-ranging, satirical panorama of Russian society in his day, rich in comic episodes and picaresque adventure. The black and paradoxical humour of *Dead Souls* is typical of Gogol's work and can seem curiously modern and ahead of its time. It is also much in evidence in his play *The Government Inspector* and in the short stories he wrote throughout his career. In one story ('The Nose') a nose takes

on a malign life of its own, independent of its possessor's will; in another ('The Overcoat') a man saves for years to buy a new coat, only to be mugged and robbed the first time he wears it. Gogol's comedy mutates easily into something dark and disturbing as it does, most notably, in 'Diary of a Madman' which records, in his own words, the descent into insanity of a petty civil servant, gradually convinced that he is the heir to the throne of Spain. Gogol's own mental health was itself unstable. In his last years he became intensely and morbidly religious and his death is thought to have been brought on by the fasting and mortification he inflicted on his body. Before his death he burned the manuscript of a further part of *Dead Souls*, on which he had been working for years, because he had decided it was sinful, but the original work lives on as one of the classics of 19th-century Russian fiction.

⮒ Read on

Diary of a Madman
Mikhail Bulgakov, *The Master and Margarita*; ❯❯ Franz Kafka, *The Castle*; Mikhail Saltykov-Shchedrin, *The Golovlyov Family*

IVAN GONCHAROV (1812–91) Russia

OBLOMOV (1859)

Ivan Goncharov worked for 30 years as a civil servant but he also pursued a parallel career as a writer, publishing his first novel in 1847 and gaining success as a travel writer before the appearance of his best-known work, *Oblomov*, a fictional portrait of a man whose function in life and society has become a mystery both to himself and to others. The book's eponymous 'hero' is a good and kind man but he is incapable of action (for the first part of the book, he cannot even persuade himself to get out of bed) and he wastes his life in idleness and inertia. His estates are plunged into financial chaos but Oblomov, stranded in St Petersburg and barely capable of contemplating a long journey into the country, let alone undertaking it, does nothing to solve the problem. Supposed friends take advantage of him but he cannot bring himself even to protect his own interests. He has been in love but his fiancée wearied of waiting for Oblomov to make decisions about their future together and broke off their engagement. Now caught in a comically ambivalent relationship of mutual dependency with his grumpy servant Zakhar, Oblomov is fretfully caged in a crumbling ruin of an apartment. Life has passed him by and, although he does eventually marry and father a son, his potential is never fulfilled. Long a classic in Russia, where 'Oblomov' has entered the language as a term to describe someone as slothful as the book's central character, the novel deserves to be more widely known in the English-speaking world. 'Oblomovitis' is a disease that afflicts people everywhere and Goncharov's funny and touching story of a good man paralysed by his own indolence transcends the particular circumstances in which it was written to have universal appeal.

🕮 Read on

The Precipice

>> Fyodor Dostoevsky, *Notes From Underground*; >> Nikolai Gogol, *Dead Souls*; >> Ivan Turgenev, *A House of Gentlefolk*

GRAHAM GREENE (1904–91) UK

BRIGHTON ROCK (1938)

Pinkie is a teenage gangster in the criminal underworld of 1930s Brighton. Fred Hale is journalist who has inadvertently incurred Pinkie's wrath and is now in fear of his life. When Pinkie does indeed assault Hale, the older man dies of a heart attack. Only the blowsy, life-loving Ida Arnold, with whom Hale had spent some of his last day, is suspicious of the circumstances surrounding the journalist's death and she tries to track down the truth behind it. Meanwhile, Pinkie realizes that evidence exists that could lead to him and that the only way to protect himself is to court and marry the young waitress Rose who, unknowingly, possesses it. As Ida closes in on Pinkie's gang and Pinkie overcomes his aversion to women in order to win Rose, the narrative moves towards a sequence of terrible events and illusion-shattering revelations. In one sense, *Brighton Rock*, like many of the books Greene labelled his 'entertainments', is a straightforward thriller, but it is complicated by the Roman Catholicism that underpins the plot. Pinkie is Catholic and believes firmly in damnation and the torments of hell (he is less certain about heaven) and so too is Rose, who knows that the suicide which Pinkie at one point in the novel urges upon her is a mortal sin. *Brighton Rock* is a novel in which the moral drama matters as much as the twists and turns of the plot. Greene, one of the most widely admired English novelists of the 20th century, produced a wide range of fiction in his life, from the mordant satire of the world of espionage in *Our Man in Havana* to the bleak analysis of a doomed relationship that is *The End of the Affair* but he published nothing that holds readers' attentions better than *Brighton Rock*, with its relentless intensity and dark ironies.

📽 **Film version:** *Brighton Rock* (starring Richard Attenborough as Pinkie, 1947)

📚 **Read on**
The End of the Affair; *The Heart of the Matter*; *The Power and the Glory*

H. RIDER HAGGARD (1856–1925) UK

KING SOLOMON'S MINES (1885)

Drawing on the knowledge of Africa he had gained during six years in the colonial service, and on the wild and romantic imagination that lurked beneath his apparently conventional exterior, Rider Haggard wrote one of the greatest of all adventure stories in *King Solomon's Mines*. The novel's three upstanding Victorian heroes (Sir Henry Curtis, Captain John Good and the narrator, the great white hunter Allan Quatermain) venture into a mysterious African kingdom in search of the treasure of King Solomon's Mines and the truth about what happened to Curtis's missing brother. There they confront its ruler, the villainous King Twala, and the deformed and treacherous witch-doctor Gagool. By a remarkable chance, their native servant, the noble Umbopa, turns out to be the rightful ruler of this lost land of the Kukuanas and Haggard's heroes must fight a civil war and overcome the trickery of Gagool in order to win him his inheritance. Two years after *King Solomon's Mines*, Haggard published another successful but improbable yarn in *She*, the story of a further forgotten African realm, ruled by an ageless and beautiful queen who possesses the secret of eternal life, and he continued to produce his exotic romances until the end of his life. None quite matched the verve and vividness of his first novel. Haggard was very much a man of his times but his books are far from being simple-minded or racist in their portraits of Africa and imperial adventure. He had, for example, a genuine fascination with, and knowledge of, Zulu culture and the novels featuring Allan Quatermain (there were several sequels) reflect this. Its pages filled with the hidden kingdoms and lost tribes of which explorers of darkest Africa dreamed and with the deeds of manly derring-do they all admired, *King Solomon's Mines* is the archetypal adventure story of the high Victorian era.

🎞 **Film versions:** *King Solomon's Mines* (with Stewart Granger as Quatermain, 1950); *King Solomon's Mines* (with Richard Chamberlain as Quatermain, 1985)

🐦 **Read on**

Allan Quatermain; *Montezuma's Daughter*; *She*

John Buchan, *Prester John*; Edgar Wallace, *Sanders of the River* (a more populist and simple-minded version of the meeting between African culture and European imperialists)

PATRICK HAMILTON (1904–62) UK

HANGOVER SQUARE (1941)

Subtitled 'A Story of Darkest Earl's Court', *Hangover Square* is the finest novel by one of the most under-rated and interesting English novelists of the 20th century. George Harvey Bone is a self-hating habitué of the cheap pubs and restaurants of Earl's Court, held there by his obsessive love for the tart and would-be actress Netta Longdon. He is also a schizophrenic who has periods in which he enters an almost trance-like state. During these 'dumb moods', as another character calls them, love for Netta turns to murderous hatred and he can think only of killing both her and one of the pub hangers-on who is her occasional lover. Bone emerges from a 'dumb mood' with little or no recollection of what he has done and said in it but with only a desperate yearning to escape the life he is leading. Each time Netta, who has learned that one of George's friends works for a theatrical agent and is thus prepared to encourage his dog-like devotion, lures him back into the same old round of boozy nights and hungover mornings. The inevitable tragedy beckons. Patrick Hamilton published his first novel in his early twenties and, in the 1930s, he became a highly successful playwright whose greatest box-office triumph, *Rope*, was filmed by Hitchcock in the 1940s and is still revived today. In 1937, he was involved in a serious car accident in a street off Earl's Court Road, from which he never fully recovered. Always a heavy drinker, he was for the rest of his life, as his friend and admirer J.B. Priestley noted, 'an unhappy man who needs whisky as a car needs petrol'. Out of his own unhappiness and addiction he fashioned a dark and compelling tale of shallow lives lived at the margins of society.

🎬 **Film version:** *Hangover Square* (1945)

📖 **Read on**
The Slaves of Solitude; *Twenty Thousand Streets Under the Sky*
➤➤ Graham Greene, *The End of the Affair*; Gerald Kersh, *Night and the City*; Julian Maclaren Ross, *Of Love and Hunger*

KNUT HAMSUN (1859–1952) Norway

HUNGER (1890)

The Norwegian writer Knut Hamsun won the Nobel Prize for Literature in 1920 but his support for Nazi ideas, when he was an old man, has tarnished his reputation and contributed to the undeserved neglect of much of his work since his death. The work which was specifically mentioned in Hamsun's Nobel citation was *Growth of the Soil*, an epic story of a small rural community in Norway and of lives ruled by the cycle of the seasons. Perhaps the novel which best represents his unique and original vision of the world, though, is *Hunger*. This story, told as a first person narration, of a starving and homeless writer in Christiania (Oslo), was the work which first made his name. 'It was in those days when I wandered about hungry in Christiania, that strange city which no one leaves before it has set its mark upon him,' the novel begins and readers witness the narrator's wanderings, his brief encounters on the streets and his frenzied attempts to write, all seen from his own peculiar and possibly deluded perspective. Grandiose plans for the world-shattering works he is going to write drift through his mind. He invents lies and stories to explain his poverty and shabby appearance to others and to himself. He descends into pits of self-loathing and self-castigation or rails against a world which is indifferent to his sufferings and his desires. And all the time starvation gnaws away at his physical and mental well-being. In its bitter evocation of life on the streets, *Hunger* echoes the naturalist novels of writers like ›› Zola. In its unravelling of the tortured psychology of its alienated narrator it anticipates many of the themes and concerns of 20th-century fiction.

Hunger remains a highly powerful and disturbing portrait of a self disintegrating under stress.

📚 Read on
Growth of the Soil; *Mysteries*; *The Women at the Pump*
Louis-Ferdinand Céline, *Journey to the End of the Night*; ›› Fyodor Dostoevsky, *Notes From the Underground*; ›› Hermann Hesse, *Steppenwolf*

THOMAS HARDY (1840–1928) UK

THE RETURN OF THE NATIVE (1878)
Hardy, the son of a builder, was born in Dorset and began his career as an architect, but his first novel (*Desperate Remedies*) was published in 1871 and he was soon earning far more from his fiction than from his architecture. Books like *Under the Greenwood Tree*, *A Pair of Blue Eyes* and *Far From the Madding Crowd* followed and established his reputation. *The Return of the Native*, like nearly all of Hardy's novels, is set in Wessex, his disguised version of the West Country in which he grew up. The native of the title is Clym Yeobright, a Wessex man who has been living in Paris, and the place to which he returns is the wild landscape of Egdon Heath. There he marries the passionate and restless Eustacia Vye who dreams of a world beyond the Heath and imagines

that Clym might take her to it. He, however, is happy to have returned to his native land and to be close to his widowed mother and he has no intention of leaving again. He has his own plans for the future. In despair, and with her dreams of escaping the Heath apparently dashed forever, Eustacia again takes up with an old lover, Damon Wildeve, who has married Clym's cousin, Thomasin. One night, when she is in her house with Wildeve, Eustacia refuses entry to Clym's mother and, as a consequence, is the inadvertent cause of her death. Eustacia and Clym separate and the scene is set for a tragic climax as she and Wildeve plan, one stormy night, to escape the Heath. *The Return of the Native* is one of Hardy's most powerful novels – a compelling narrative in which the brooding presence of Egdon Heath hangs over all the characters, seeming to force them into the fates that await them.

🕮 Read on

Far From the Madding Crowd; *The Mayor of Casterbridge*
John Cowper Powys, *Wolf Solent*; Mary Webb, *Precious Bane*

TESS OF THE D'URBERVILLES (1891)

Tess Durbeyfield, the daughter of a local village carrier, is brought up in the belief that her family is descended from one of ancient renown and that the local squires, the Stoke D'Urbervilles, are somehow distant kin. The only result of this Durbeyfield dreaming is that Tess is seduced by Alec D'Urberville and then swiftly abandoned when she becomes pregnant. Tess's baby dies and she is obliged to move away from her home village to escape wagging tongues. Working on a farm in a different part of Wessex, she meets and falls in love with Angel Clare but, after their wedding, she feels obliged to confess her past. Clare responds with pious horror to the news that Tess is not the 'pure' woman he thought and leaves the country for South America. Tess is once again pursued by Alec but, when Angel returns from his self-imposed exile a wiser man, prepared to accept his wife's past, she is placed in a desperate dilemma that leads inexorably to tragedy. *Tess of the D'Urbervilles* was to be one of Hardy's final novels. By choosing the subtitle 'A Pure Woman' for a novel in which the heroine has an illegitimate child, he was throwing the gauntlet down to the guardians of Victorian sexual mores and many reviewers responded with outrage. Wearied by the criticisms and accusations of immorality levelled at the book and, particularly, at *Jude the Obscure*, published four years later, Hardy gave up fiction and returned to his first love, poetry, producing many volumes of verse over the last 30 years of his life. Today, Hardy's relative frankness about sex (for the time) and his criticism of hypocritical condemnation of women like Tess seems very mild but, if the novel is now unlikely to arouse moral outrage, it none the less retains its power as one of the great tragic stories of Victorian literature.

Film version: *Tess* (directed by Roman Polanski, Nastassja Kinski as Tess 1979)

Read on
Jude the Obscure; *The Woodlanders*
>> Edith Wharton, *Ethan Frome*

READONATHEME: LADIES WHO LAPSED

>> Kate Chopin, *The Awakening*
>> George Eliot, *Adam Bede*
>> Theodor Fontane, *Effi Briest*
>> Ford Madox Ford, *The Good Soldier*
>> Nathaniel Hawthorne, *The Scarlet Letter*
>> D.H. Lawrence, *Lady Chatterley's Lover*
Rabindranath Tagore, *The Home and the World*
F. Tennyson Jesse, *A Pin to See the Peepshow*
>> Émile Zola, *Thérèse Raquin*

JAROSLAV HAŠEK (1883–1923) Czech Republic

THE GOOD SOLDIER SVEJK

Hašek's comic masterpiece, unfinished at the time of his early death, reflects its author's own boozy, disorganized life. Born in Prague, Hašek was a journalist there before the First World War but his drinking and his independent spirit meant that he rarely held a job for any length of time. He worked on an anarchist newspaper but was sacked for stealing the office bicycle. For a while he edited a magazine called *Animal World* but was again shown the door when it was discovered that he had been inventing animals, otherwise unknown to zoology, and writing articles about them. His most famous character, Svejk, made his first appearance in print in 1912 but it was the Great War that provided the opportunity for both character and author to flourish. Hašek's anti-hero is a clueless conscript into the Austrian army whose farcical career the novel follows. Svejk is no rebel or revolutionary. His only interest is in the basic comforts of life – food, drink and somewhere to rest his head at the end of the day. He is, if anything, over-eager to please. Give him an order and he follows it with unswerving literalness. His lack of initiative and unthinking willingness to obey any instruction, no matter how fatuous it might be, leads to far more disorder than the most reckless of rebels could possibly instigate. Sleepwalking through war and revolution and the mindless bureaucracy of the army, immune to calls to patriotism and military glory and determined only to survive, Svejk leaves a trail of chaos in his wake. Drawing on his own anarchic spirit and his own experiences in the First World War (he fought in the front line and was captured by the Russians), Hašek produced one of the great comic novels of the 20th century, an epic and very funny chronicle of one bumbling man's progress through the insanity of war.

🕮 Read on

The Red Commissar (a selection, first published in the 1980s, of Hašek's shorter works, including further exploits of Svejk)
Joseph Heller, *Catch-22*; Bohumil Hrabal, *I Served the King of England*; Vladimir Voinovich, *The Life and Extraordinary Adventures of Private Ivan Chonkin*

NATHANIEL HAWTHORNE (1804–64) USA

THE SCARLET LETTER (1850)

Hawthorne came from a well-known and long-established New England family and he was a direct descendant of one of the judges in the infamous Salem witch trial of the late 17th century. His mixture of pride in his ancestry and abhorrence of the intolerant Puritanism that it embodied fuelled much of his fiction, from short stories such as 'Young Goodman Brown' and 'The Maypole of Merry Mount' to *The Scarlet Letter*, his best-known work. Set in 17th-century Boston, the novel has as its central character a young woman named Hester Prynne who, when the main narrative opens, has been condemned for adultery and forced to wear the 'scarlet letter' of the title, an 'A' embroidered on her clothes, to mark her out as a sinner. Hester had travelled from England ahead of her elderly husband and, when he failed to arrive in the New World, seemingly lost at sea, she took a lover and became pregnant. She refuses to name her lover and she and her child, Pearl, become outcasts in the community. A man calling himself Roger Chillingworth, in reality Hester's missing husband, arrives in Boston in time to witness her disgrace and he vows to discover the identity of the lover and have his revenge. His suspicion falls on the Reverend Arthur Dimmesdale and, as the years pass, he worms his way into the minister's household and adds additional torments to the guilt and remorse that Dimmesdale is already suffering. While Hester redeems her 'sin' by living a virtuous and Christian life, her husband and her lover pursue a bitter enmity which damages both themselves and nearly everyone with whom they come into contact. In Hawthorne's powerful vision of

New England in the early years of its settlement, it is the life-denying Puritan morality of the men rather than Hester's brief adultery that stands condemned.

 Film version: *The Scarlet Letter* (with Demi Moore as Hester and Gary Oldman as Dimmesdale, 1995)

 Read on
The Blithedale Romance; *The House of the Seven Gables*
Charles Brockden Brown, *Wieland*

ERNEST HEMINGWAY (1898–1961) USA

A FAREWELL TO ARMS (1929)

Frederic Henry is an American ambulance driver in Italy during the last years of the First World War who meets a young English nurse, Catherine Barkley. They embark on a playful game of love in which neither of them invests too much emotion but, when Frederic is wounded and Catherine becomes his carer, their feelings intensify. She becomes pregnant. Frederic, now recovered, must return to the Front where he experiences the chaos and misery of the Italian retreat from Caporetto. Utterly disgusted by the madness and violence of war, he deserts and he and Catherine flee to neutral Switzerland. Happiness seems to beckon for both of them but fate has a cruel trick up its sleeve. The book draws extensively on Hemingway's own experiences when he came to Europe as a young man to serve in an ambulance unit during the First World War. Like Frederic Henry, Hemingway was wounded and, like him, he began an intense, short-lived relationship with the woman who nursed him. In the decades of his greatest fame, Hemingway's terse and mini-malist prose style, so distinctive and influential, was parodied and imitated so often that it is difficult today to appreciate just how revolu-tionary it seemed in the 1920s. With its precision and its deliberate avoidance of over-complication, it seemed to herald a new honesty and directness in fiction. In later years, Hemingway himself drifted perilously close to self-parody but the novels and short stories of the 1920s are the real thing. *A Farewell to Arms*, more than other equally well-known Hemingway books such as the Spanish Civil War novel *For Whom the Bell Tolls* and the Pulitzer Prize-winning novella *The Old Man and the Sea*, shows just why he was one of the great innovatory American writers of the 20th century.

 Film versions: *A Farewell to Arms* (with Gary Cooper as Frederic, 1932); *A Farewell to Arms* (with Rock Hudson as Frederic, 1957)

 Read on
For Whom the Bell Tolls; *The Old Man and the Sea*
John Dos Passos, *Three Soldiers*; ›› F. Scott Fitzgerald, *Tender is the Night*; Michael Ondaatje, *The English Patient*

HERMANN HESSE (1877–1962) Germany

NARZISS AND GOLDMUND (1930)

The gentle mysticism of much of Hesse's work, combined with his interests in Jungian ideas about archetypes and the collective unconscious and Buddhist philosophy, made him a novelist ideally suited to the spirit of the 1960s and his fiction won new admirers in that decade. Forty years later, his books can be seen to possess much more than just the rather woolly qualities that appealed in the Summer of Love. Hesse was a more tough-minded and rewarding writer than his reputation sometimes suggests. *The Glass Bead Game*, set in a future society governed by an elaborate game, is a powerful and imaginative examination of the relationship between the intellect, the emotions and the world in which we live. *Steppenwolf* is a gripping portrait of a man struggling to reconcile different sides of his divided personality. Hesse's 1930 novel *Narziss and Goldmund* is, however, his most profound exploration of the divided human self and its desire for integrity. Set in medieval Germany, it dramatizes the conflict between the flesh and the spirit in the two characters that give the book its title. Narziss is an ascetic monk and teacher, committed to the life of the mind and the spirit. Goldmund is a young man who enters the monastery as a novice in search of the best way to live his life. Narziss recognizes that Goldmund is a sensualist, not suited to monastic isolation, and that, despite his wish to stay in the monastery and dedicate his life to God, his destiny lies outside the cloister. Much of the novel traces Goldmund's wanderings once he leaves the monastery and the experiences in the world that gradually bring him to the kind of wisdom that his friend Narziss can only achieve by withdrawing from it. Through the contrasting characters of Narziss and Goldmund, Hesse investigates ideas about carnality and spirituality which underpin all his finest work.

🕮 Read on

The Glass Bead Game; *Steppenwolf*

Heinrich Böll, *The Clown*; ▸▸ Knut Hamsun, *Mysteries*; ▸▸ Thomas Mann, *The Holy Sinner*

JAMES HOGG (1770–1835) UK

THE PRIVATE MEMOIRS AND CONFESSIONS OF A JUSTIFIED SINNER (1824)

In his own lifetime, Hogg, a self-taught writer from a poor rural background, was best known as a poet. Championed by ▸▸ Sir Walter Scott and other leading figures from the literary world, he was seen as an untutored rustic genius in the tradition established by Robert Burns. Several volumes of his verse were published, but none of these proved any preparation for his masterpiece, the strange gothic tale of Robert Wringhim, a religious fanatic egged on to murder by an enigmatic alter ego who may or may not be the Devil. Like ▸▸ Stevenson's *The Strange Case of Dr Jekyll and Mr Hyde*, which it strongly influenced, Hogg's novel makes use of different narratives to tell what is ultimately seen as the same story. In the first, an 'editor' presents the story of the murder of Wringhim's half-brother George Colwan; in the second, readers see events from Wringhim's perspective and hear how his *doppelgänger* persuades him that, in a universe where (as the Calvinist Wringhim believes) God has already chosen those souls who are saved, there is nothing he can do which will affect his predestined salvation. Since Wringhim cannot achieve salvation through his deeds, and his fate is predestined, it matters little whether what he does is good or evil in the world's eye. Ambiguities and ironies pervade the pages of Hogg's strange and powerful novel. Readers are never quite sure of what to believe or not to believe in the narrative. Is the devil-like tempter intended to be real (at the end of the book it seems that, after death, Wringhim has been finally claimed by the forces of evil) or are readers to assume from the very beginning that he is a figment of Wringhim's imagination, a projection of his own darkest desires? Mixing psychological insights which seem remarkably modern with age-old ideas about demonic possession, Hogg produced one of the most original and chilling novels of the 19th century.

⮁ Read on

William Godwin, *Caleb Williams*; Mary Shelley, *Frankenstein*; ⟩⟩ Robert Louis Stevenson, *The Strange Case of Dr Jekyll and Mr Hyde*

VICTOR HUGO (1802–85) France

LES MISÉRABLES (1862)

In France, Victor Hugo is recognized as one of the most influential writers of the 19th century and one of the country's greatest novelists and poets. Outside France, he is remembered for two novels. One is the historical narrative *The Hunchback of Notre Dame*, first published in 1831 and set in the medieval period, which tells of the doomed love of the deformed bell-ringer Quasimodo for the beautiful Esmeralda. The other is *Les Misérables*, an epic indictment of social injustice and the law, which appeared 30 years later. Many people know *Les Misérables* and its story of the noble convict, Valjean, relentlessly pursued by the policeman Javert, but they know it from the musical rather than the novel. Victor Hugo's original work, although long and often weighted down by the kind of philosophical digressions so many 19th-century novelists loved, is worth discovering. Jean Valjean serves a long prison sentence after stealing food for his starving family and, when he is released, he finds that the world is still against him. Turning once again to crime, he steals from a clergyman who gives him shelter but the clergyman protects him from the consequences with the proviso that he must become a reformed character. Under a new identity, Valjean prospers but his past catches up with him and he is obliged to flee to Paris, accompanied by a young girl, Cosette, for whom he has taken responsibility. The years pass and still the law, in the shape of Javert, pursues him. Cosette grows up and falls in love with a young student. In the violence and chaos of the July Revolution of 1830, as the barricades are erected on the streets of Paris and the students riot, the story of Valjean, Javert and Cosette reaches its climax.

📖 **Film versions:** *Les Misérables* (with Fredric March and Charles Laughton, 1935); *Les Misérables* (with Liam Neeson, 1998)

📚 **Read on**
The Hunchback of Notre Dame
›› Charles Dickens, *Bleak House*

ALDOUS HUXLEY (1894–1963) UK

EYELESS IN GAZA (1936)

Best remembered today for *Brave New World*, his dystopian vision of a biologically engineered future, and for his experiments with psychedelic drugs (*The Doors of Perception*), Huxley was known in the 1920s and 1930s as the author of erudite and mordantly witty satires of contemporary life. *Eyeless in Gaza* is a novel that charts the career of its central character, Anthony Beavis, from his childhood and adolescence through his experiences as a member of the intellectual elite of inter-war London to a journey to Mexico which opens his eyes to the real values of life. Huxley himself wrote that the novel is about 'what happens to someone who becomes really very free' and that it records 'the rather awful vacuum that such freedom turns out to be'. Beavis is a man who appears to be liberated. He is comfortably off and therefore freed from the fear of poverty and the inconvenience of uncongenial work. He is intellectually gifted and able to free himself from the chains of conventional thinking. His sexual life is one of cool promiscuity, freed from commitment and the constraints of commonplace morality. Yet, beneath the surface, he is emotionally scarred by the death of his mother when he was a child and by the suicide of his closest friend for which he considers himself partly responsible. Apparently the luckiest of men, he has lost any sense of purpose in his own life and meaning in the wider universe. 'Simply to be shaken out of negativity', he decides to accompany a Communist friend to Mexico to join the revolution in that country and there, despite the disasters that overtake the two men, he finds his life is changed. Samson in Milton's poem *Samson Agonistes*, from which Huxley takes his title, is physically blind. Beavis is metaphorically blind and Huxley's narrative, moving backwards and forwards in time, reveals the process by which he gains his sight.

≋ Read on

Antic Hay; *Point Counter Point*

➤➤ F. Scott Fitzgerald, *Tender is the Night*; Eric Linklater, *Juan in America*; Anthony Powell, *What's Become of Waring?*

HENRY JAMES (1843–1916) USA/UK

THE PORTRAIT OF A LADY (1881)

Henry James, born in New York City, settled in London in 1876, the year his first major novel, *Roderick Hudson*, was published, and lived in the city for the next twenty years. He moved to Rye on the south coast in the late 1890s and, having spent much of his adult life in England, he finally became a naturalized British citizen in the year before his death. Henry James's great subject as a novelist was the meeting and mingling of the old world and the new, the interactions between those brought up in the centuries-long culture of Europe and those brought up amid the brash vitality of 19th-century America. None of his novels embodies this better than *The Portrait of a Lady*. The lady in question is Isabel Archer, a young woman from New England who is brought to Europe by her aunt. After the death of her uncle, a retired banker who provides for her in his will, Isabel becomes a wealthy woman. Her inheritance excites the attention of Gilbert Osmond, a selfish and cynical aesthete in search of a way to marry into money. Aided and abetted by his long-term mistress, Madame Merle, Osmond exercises his charm on Isabel and they eventually become husband and wife. The marriage is doomed from the start by Osmond's egotism and lack of any real feelings for Isabel and, in a sequence of devastating revelations, she is forced to face the fact that, despite the independent spirit on which she has always prided herself, she has been duped by the scheming of Osmond and Madame Merle. With its multi-layered ironies, its careful studies of American lives lived in Europe and its subtle examination of a woman who tries but fails to shape her own future, *The Portrait of a Lady* is one of Henry James's most effective and moving novels.

📽 **Film version:** *The Portrait of a Lady* (with Nicole Kidman as Isabel and John Malkovich as Osmond, 1996)

📖 **Read on**
Roderick Hudson; *Washington Square*
>> Elizabeth Bowen, *The Death of the Heart*; >> Edith Wharton, *Madame de Treymes*

THE WINGS OF THE DOVE (1902)

Kate Croy is a young woman obliged by genteel poverty to live with her rich and snobbish aunt, Mrs Lowder, who plans that Kate should marry into money. Kate herself has other ideas and is already secretly engaged to a journalist named Merton Densher. Milly Theale is a rich young American, slowly succumbing to a fatal illness, who arrives in London and becomes Kate's friend. Kate, however, sees in Milly a means of solving her problems and of giving herself the opportunity to marry Densher and to be happy. When Milly, advised by her doctor that she should travel, journeys to Venice and takes up residence in a decaying *palazzo* on the Grand Canal, Kate encourages her fiancé to follow her and to woo her in the hope that they can marry. Milly's last months will be made happy and, after her death, Densher will be a rich widower. He and Kate can then marry and live in comfort. The deception, which Kate convinces herself is harmless and to the benefit of everyone, is revealed through the spitefulness of another of Milly's suitors and leads to tragedy for every one of the main characters. Henry James's later novels are often said to be over-elaborated and difficult to read but *The Wings of the Dove* shows how wrong this judgement is.

James takes the relatively simple, even melodramatic, story of an inno-cent young woman, facing early death and vulnerable to the exploitation of those more worldly and ruthless than she is, and turns it into a subtle and moving analysis of what the true value of life is. It is not always an easy read – the density and complexity of James's prose in which more is always going on beneath the surface than first appears can makes demands on the reader – but it is ultimately a rewarding one.

🎬 **Film version:** *The Wings of the Dove* (with Helena Bonham Carter as Kate, 1997)

📚 **Read on**
The Ambassadors; *The Golden Bowl*
>> Ford Madox Ford, *The Good Soldier*; **>>** Edith Wharton, *The Reef*

JAMES JOYCE (1882–1941) Ireland

ULYSSES (1922)

James Joyce was born and brought up in Dublin but he left the city in 1902 and, apart from a period immediately following his mother's death the following year, he returned rarely and never for very long. His most famous novel, a vast reconstruction of one day in Dublin, was a work of memory, as Joyce, in self-imposed exile on the continent, re-imagined the city of his youth. *Ulysses* deals with the events of 16 June 1904 (the day on which Joyce, in real life, had taken his first walk with Nora Barnacle, his future wife) and the experiences on that date of the two central characters, Stephen Dedalus, Joyce's own literary alter ego, and Leopold Bloom, a part-Jewish advertising salesman who is Joyce's everyman hero. These are ordinary and unexceptional – they shave, go to the toilet, eat, drink, argue in bars, go to a funeral, borrow money, flirt with girls on a beach, visit the city's red-light district – but they are given a heroic status by the parallels with Homer's *Odyssey* and made vivid by the stream of consciousness techniques Joyce uses to bring their inner thoughts and feelings to life. Each of the ordinary events of the day is a launching pad for Joyce's extraordinary plunges into the minds of his characters. Packed with puns and parodies, fragmentary quotations from other works of literature, shaggy dog stories and dirty jokes, Joyce's style is unique and *Ulysses*, which ends with a bravura 60-page monologue from Bloom's unfaithful wife Molly, her thoughts as she drifts off to sleep beside her husband, is a book like no other. No other novel has ever celebrated the pains and pleasures of the everyday world and the inner life of its characters with such attentiveness, wit and joy in the power of language.

🎬 **Film version:** *Ulysses* (1967)

🍴 **Read on**
Dubliners; *Portrait of the Artist as a Young Man*
Samuel Beckett, *Molloy*; **»** Flann O'Brien, *At Swim-Two-Birds*; **»**
Laurence Sterne, *Tristram Shandy*

FRANZ KAFKA (1883–1924) Czech Republic

THE TRIAL (1925)

Little of Kafka's writing was published in his lifetime and he was hardly known outside a small circle of friends, one of whom, Max Brod, was largely responsible for preserving and publishing the manuscripts that Kafka left when he died from tuberculosis at the age of only 41. *The Trial* first appeared in German the year after its author's death. Joseph K., the central character in Kafka's nightmarish narrative, awakes one morning to find that he is under arrest. No one will tell him the crimes of which he is accused and never, in the course of the interrogation to which he is subjected, is it explained. Events move relentlessly towards a seemingly inevitable and violent conclusion. Kafka is one of those novelists who has had an adjective coined from his name and the description 'Kafkaesque' is regularly given to any fiction in which characters struggle against faceless bureaucracy and an apparently malign fate. Just as Byron was more than just Byronic and Dickens wrote novels which were not simply Dickensian, Kafka was a much more wide-ranging writer than the usually accepted meaning of Kafkaesque suggests. His work, particularly his short stories, contain far more than just gloomy alienation and paranoia. There is a grotesque comedy in many of the stories, from 'Metamorphosis', with its famous account of a man struggling to deal with the fact that he has been transformed overnight into a gigantic beetle, to 'In the Penal Colony', where a prison officer is so impressed by a new device for torture and execution that he eventually uses it on himself. The novels, particularly *The Trial*, may seem open to interpretation as dark political allegories, predictive of the fascist horrors that were soon to engulf much of Europe, but they can also be read as daring exercises in the blackest of black humour.

🎞 **Film versions:** *The Trial* (directed by Orson Welles, with Anthony Perkins as Joseph K., 1962); *The Trial* (1993)

📚 **Read on**
The Castle; *Metamorphosis and Other Stories*
›› Albert Camus, *The Fall*; ›› George Orwell, *1984*; Rex Warner, *The Aerodrome*

RUDYARD KIPLING (1865–1936) India/UK

KIM (1901)

Born in Bombay, where his father was teaching in an art school, Kipling was sent to school in England, an experience he hated, but returned to the land of his birth to begin his career as a journalist in Lahore. He was already, as a very young man, writing and publishing verse and short sketches so that, when he ventured back to England in 1889, he was poised to make his name in the literary world. *Barrack Room Ballads*, a collection of poems which established his reputation as a master of vernacular verse, was followed by several volumes of short stories and by *The Jungle Book*. His best-known novel, *Kim*, was published a decade after Kipling had last seen India but it is his finest tribute to the tumultuous richness of the land of his birth. Kimball O'Hara is the orphaned son of an Irish sergeant serving in India who lives a precarious life on the streets of Lahore. In his attempts to escape the beggary that fate seems to have assigned him, Kim becomes both the disciple of a wandering Tibetan lama and, later, an agent in the British secret service engaged in the 'Great Game' of imperial espionage against the Russians. Successful as a spy and yet drawn to the lama's quest to be freed from the Wheel of Life, Kim is torn between the conflicting demands of the life of action and the life of the spirit. In the course of Kim's adventures, Kipling treats his readers to an extraordinarily rich portrait of the sights, sounds and people of India. He went on to win the Nobel Prize for Literature in 1907 and to publish many further volumes of verse and short stories (including *Puck of Pook's Hill* and *Rewards and Fairies*) but *Kim* remained perhaps his finest achievement.

◈ **Film version:** *Kim* (with Dean Stockwell as Kim and a cast that includes Errol Flynn, 1950)

≋ **Read on**
Captains Courageous; *Soldiers Three* (stories); *Stalky and Co.*
J.G. Farrell, *The Siege of Krishnapur*; M.M. Kaye, *The Far Pavilions*;
John Masters, *The Lotus and the Wind*

CHODERLOS DE LACLOS (1741–1803) France

DANGEROUS LIAISONS (1782)

Choderlos de Laclos was a French soldier and minor aristocrat who dabbled in literature (before writing *Dangerous Liaisons*, his greatest literary triumph had been the libretto for a comic opera) and wrote his great epistolary novel as a cool, unsensational exposé of the corrupt sexual morality of the pre-Revolutionary upper classes in France. At the heart of the story is the libertine Vicomte de Valmont who plots to seduce the virtuous wife of Monsieur de Tourvel. His female counterpart is the Marquise de Merteuil who, in pursuit of revenge on a former lover, incites Valmont to exercise his powers of sexual persuasion on the innocent young girl her ex-lover is engaged to marry. The narrative, revealed through the characters' correspondence, follows the heartless scheming of Valmont and the Marquise as they entangle those less sophisticated than themselves in their lies and deceit. The epistolary novel, in which the story unfolds through letters, was a popular genre of fiction in the 18th century, both in France and in England where Samuel Richardson, in lengthy works such as *Pamela and Clarissa*, used the form to narrate tales of virtue staunchly defending itself against vice. Laclos's novel is more cynical, more realistic and less concerned with extracting a moral from its story than anything Richardson ever wrote but the Frenchman employed the genre, and the opportunity it provided to use different narrative voices, with just as much skill. *Dangerous Liaisons* was his one great triumph in literature. Throughout the dangerous years of the French Revolution, he continued his career as a soldier and he ended his life as a Napoleonic general. His military successes, such as they were, have long been forgotten but his unsentimental portrait of an unscrupulous seducer and his accomplice, rich in psychological insight, lives on.

◢ Film versions: *Les Liaisons Dangereuses* (directed by Roger Vadim, with Jeanne Moreau as the Marquise, 1959); *Dangerous Liaisons* (Glenn Close and John Malkowich as the scheming pair, Michelle Pfeiffer as Madame de Tourvel, 1988); *Valmont* (directed by Milos Forman, with Colin Firth, Annette Bening and Meg Tilly, 1989)

≋ Read on

Abbé Prévost, *Manon Lescaut*; Jean-Jacques Rousseau, *Julie or the New Heloïse*; Samuel Richardson, *Clarissa*

D.H. LAWRENCE (1885–1930) UK

SONS AND LOVERS (1913)

Born in Eastwood, Nottinghamshire, the son of a coalminer, Lawrence studied at the local university and taught as an elementary school teacher before publishing his first novel in 1911. The largely auto-biographical *Sons and Lovers* followed two years later. Lawrence's *alter ego* in the novel is Paul Morel, whose over-protective mother is fiercely determined that her son should not follow his father down the pits. Gertrude Morel's heavy emotional investment in her second son, even more concentrated after the death of his older brother William, has a profound effect on his relationship with the other women in his life. Miriam Leivers, the daughter of a local farmer who encourages his dreams of being a painter, and Clara Dawes, the married woman with whom he conducts a passionate but ultimately unsatisfactory affair, are unable to compete with the hold Gertrude continues to exert on her adult son. Only by breaking free of his mother's influence can Paul gain true independence and the emotional price he pays is a high one. Lawrence went on to write other equally powerful novels. *The Rainbow* and *Women in Love* follow the fortunes of the Brangwen family, particularly the two sisters Ursula and Gudrun, as they struggle to create relationships that are sexually and emotionally fulfilling and which do not stifle their longings for freedom and independence. In the last years of his life he gained even more notoriety than he had gathered in his earlier career with the sexual explicitness of *Lady Chatterley's Lover*, which was banned in his own lifetime and only finally published in an unexpurgated and freely available edition after a famous court case in the 1960s. However, *Sons and Lovers*, fuelled by the autobiographical intensity that brought it into being, continues to be the novel that best introduces the particular power and passion of Lawrence's fiction.

🎬 **Film version:** *Sons and Lovers* (with Trevor Howard, Wendy Hiller and Dean Stockwell, 1960)

📖 **Read on**
The Rainbow; *Women in Love*
Henry Miller, *Tropic of Cancer*

HALLDÓR LAXNESS (1902–98) Iceland

INDEPENDENT PEOPLE (1934–5)

The Icelandic writer Halldór Laxness won the 1955 Nobel Prize for Literature and, in the words of the Nobel citation, his books have a 'vivid epic power which renews the great narrative art of Iceland'. It is certainly true that Laxness's novels have much of the elemental simplicity of the medieval Icelandic sagas but they are also written with a sense of irony and ambivalence that is entirely modern. In the course of his very long life (he reached the age of 95), he published more than 50 works of fiction as well as poetry, plays and essays. These ranged from *The Fish*

Can Sing, a lyrical story of a young boy and his relationship with a reclusive opera singer who has found as much contentment in retirement as he ever found in the wider world, to *The Atom Station*, a powerful and satirical tale of a young woman's involvement in the struggle to prevent the Cold War invasion of Iceland by Americans intent on the establishment of a bomber base. Probably his greatest novel, however, is *Independent People*, set amid the remote rural communities of Iceland in the late 19th and early 20th centuries. Bjartur Jonsson, the flinty, unyielding character at the heart of the book, serves eighteen years in virtual slavery to a landowner so, when he finally gains his freedom and has his own small plot of land to cultivate, he is determined at all costs to retain the independence he has won so hardly. In doing so, ironically, he blights the lives of others around him, most particularly his daughter who longs to be free of the tyranny her father imposes on her. In Laxness's clear-sighted and rigorously unsentimental narrative, Bjartur's independence costs him as much, in human terms, as did his long years in bondage.

☜ Read on
The Fish Can Sing; *Under the Glacier*
➤➤ Knut Hamsun, *Growth of the Soil*; Jane Smiley, *The Greenlanders*

MIKHAIL LERMONTOV (1814–41) Russia

A HERO OF OUR TIME

Killed in a duel when he was only 26, Lermontov was one of the great figures of the Romantic movement in Russia, second in importance only to the national poet Pushkin. Apart from his poetry, 'iron verse steeped in bitterness and hatred' as he once described it himself, he is remembered for the novel, *A Hero of Our Time*, written two years before his death. The hero of our time is Pechorin, a self-consciously Byronic figure, sensitive and selfish, arrogant and melancholic. The novel actually consists of a number of interconnected short stories and is mostly set in the Caucasus which Lermontov, who served there as an officer of dragoons, knew well. Three narrative voices are heard in the book – an unnamed narrator who introduces two of the stories, an older officer, Maksim Maksimych, who served with Pechorin in the Caucasus and who recounts his experience of him and, finally, Pechorin himself whose cynicism and world-weariness are revealed in the pages of his own journal. Pechorin is more than half in love with death and adopts a pose of indifferent ennui in the face of it. 'If I die, I die,' he remarks at one point in the book. 'It will be no great loss to the world, and I am thoroughly bored with life. I am like a man yawning at a ball; the only reason he does not go home to bed is that his carriage has not arrived yet.' He is also a cruel and heartless pursuer of women and a man quite prepared to kill a friend in a duel. In *A Hero of Our Time*, Lermontov produced both an indictment of the follies and pretensions of the Romantic poseur which Pechorin, in one sense, is, and a tragic portrait of a man of great potential who fails to realize it and eventually achieves only the early death for which part of him craves.

⮒ Read on

⟫ Nikolai Gogol, *Taras Bulba*; Alexander Pushkin, *Eugene Onegin* (a novel in verse in which a young aristocrat cruelly rejects the love of a passionate woman only to find, years later, that the tables are turned on him); ⟫ Leo Tolstoy, *The Cossacks*; ⟫ Ivan Turgenev, *Fathers and Sons*

MALCOLM LOWRY (1909–1957) UK

UNDER THE VOLCANO (1947)

Malcolm Lowry's life was shaped by his enthralment to drink and most of it was spent on spectacular benders, in drying-out clinics where he attempted fruitlessly to beat his addiction or in long periods of exile and isolation in Mexico, Canada and the USA when he strove to turn his experiences into fiction. Apart from *Ultramarine*, which appeared soon after he graduated from Cambridge, Lowry published only one novel in his lifetime but that book is one of the most powerful and original works of English fiction in the 20th century. *Under the Volcano* traces the last 24 hours in the life of Geoffrey Firmin. Firmin, a terminally alcoholic ex-British consul living in a small Mexican town, is witness to his own destruction through drink, despair and the haunting power of his memories. Set on the festival of the Day of the Dead, the book records the *via dolorosa* that is Firmin's journey to his own death. His ex-wife, Yvonne, and his half-brother, Hugh, look on powerlessly as he soaks in liquor and self-castigation. They labour under their own burdens of guilt (the two had an affair in the past and Hugh despises himself for his unwillingness to commit himself to the great political struggles of the times) and ultimately they are unable to save either Firmin or themselves. As the macabre festival celebrating death swirls around them and fascist thugs gather in the Mexican streets, the three lost English souls are forced to face their fates. *Under the Volcano* is a remarkable achievement. Out of the messy circumstances of his own addiction, Lowry fashions a semi-autobiographical narrative that becomes symbolic of much more than just one man's troubled descent into a hell of his own making. Firmin's tragedy becomes the tragedy of everyone caught up in the suffering, violence and loneliness of the modern world.

🎞 **Film version:** *Under the Volcano* (directed by John Huston and starring Albert Finney as Firmin, 1984)

📖 **Read on**
Dark as the Grave Wherein My Friend is Laid (posthumously published); *Ultramarine*
Saul Bellow, *Humboldt's Gift*; John O'Hara, *Appointment in Samarra*; B. Traven, *The Bridge in the Jungle*

READ ON A THEME: BOOZE AND BOOZERS

    Joyce Cary, *The Horse's Mouth*
>> F. Scott Fitzgerald, *The Beautiful and Damned*
>> Graham Greene, *The Power and the Glory*
>> Patrick Hamilton, *Hangover Square*
    Charles Jackson, *The Lost Weekend*
    Jean Rhys, *Good Morning, Midnight*
>> Joseph Roth, *The Legend of the Holy Drinker*
    Budd Schulberg, *The Disenchanted*

THOMAS MANN (1875–1955) Germany

THE MAGIC MOUNTAIN (1924)

One of the greatest novelists of the 20th century, Thomas Mann was one of a dynasty of writing Manns who made their mark on German literature. Both his elder brother Heinrich and his son Klaus produced fiction, particularly during the years of the Weimar Republic, which mirrored the troubled history of Germany during the first half of the century and all the Manns were exiled from their country during the Nazi years. Thomas Mann's earliest success came with *Buddenbrooks*, published in 1901, a massive novel chronicling the decline of a rich bourgeois family in the last decades of the 19th century. In a long career, Mann wrote many masterpieces (*Doktor Faustus*, the story of a musical genius whose life echoes the Faust myth, appeared nearly half a century after *Buddenbrooks*) but his finest achievement is the long and complex *The Magic Mountain*. Like so many of the great European novels, *The Magic Mountain* chronicles the moral and intellectual education of its central character. The Germans gave a name to this genre of fiction (*Bildungsroman*) and Mann was working in a long tradition of such fiction but, in his hands, it has a power and a wide-ranging irony that is all his own. Hans Castorp is a rich but complacent young man who travels to a sanatorium in the Swiss mountains. Diagnosed with TB, his departure from the sanatorium is repeatedly delayed and eventually it becomes his home for seven years and his fellow sufferers become his guides to the art and philosophy of European high culture. Schooled by his mentors in the conflicting values of different ideologies and beliefs about the world and by Madame Cauchat in the distractions of sensual love, Castorp's years in the rarefied atmosphere of the mountains change him irrevocably. The novel's biggest irony, however, is that it takes place in the years leading up to the First World War and the culture that Castorp has so painstakingly acquired is about to ring its own death knell.

≋ Read on
Buddenbrooks; *The Confessions of Felix Krull, Confidence Man*; *Death in Venice*; *Doktor Faustus*
>> Johann Wolfgang von Goethe, *The Apprenticeship of Wilhelm Meister*; Heinrich Mann, *Man of Straw*

GUY DE MAUPASSANT (1850–93) France

BEL-AMI (1885)

Guy de Maupassant is better known for his shorter fiction than for his novels and probably his most famous short story (very nearly lengthy enough to be defined as a novella) is 'Boule de Suif', which tells of a coach journey through France during the Franco-Prussian War of 1870. Travelling on the coach to escape the fighting are several respectable members of society and a prostitute nicknamed Boule de Suif ('Suet Pudding'). The respectable passengers ignore the prostitute in their midst but she wins them over with her friendliness and humanity. The coach is stopped on its journey by a Prussian officer who demands sex from Boule de Suif as the price for allowing all of them to continue their journey. The other passengers beg her to agree and, when she does, and the coach gets underway again, they reject her once more. In the handful of novels he wrote, Maupassant exercises the same unsparing naturalism and ruthless observation of social mores that he shows in 'Boule de Suif'. Of these, the best is probably **Bel-Ami**. Reminiscent of a number of other French novels of the 19th century, from ›› Stendhal's *Scarlet and Black* to ›› Balzac's stories of provincials seeking their fortune in Paris, Maupassant's book traces the rise and rise of Georges Duroy. Duroy begins his career as a lowly clerk but he becomes a journalist and uses his wit and his charm to mount further and further up the social ladder. Owing more to his gifts as a seducer of women who can help him than to his talents as a writer, he plunges further and further into the hypocrisy and corruption that characterize the upper echelons of Parisian society. With its richly cynical and satirical portrait of its social-climbing anti-hero and the world in which he operates, *Bel-Ami* is one of the wittiest and most enjoyable of all 19th-century French novels.

📽 **Film version:** *The Private Affairs of Bel Ami* (1947)

📚 **Read on**
Pierre and Jean
›› Honoré de Balzac, *César Birotteau*; ›› Stendhal, *Scarlet and Black*; ›› Émile Zola, *His Excellency*

HERMAN MELVILLE (1819–91) USA

MOBY DICK (1851)

Now considered one of the greatest of all American novelists, Herman Melville had gained little recognition by the time of his death, and *Moby Dick*, his most ambitious work, had to wait for new generations to appreciate its power and intensity. The narrator of Melville's complex and epic novel is Ishmael who, as the book opens, has chosen to join a whaling expedition. Together with his friend Queequeg, a harpooner from a South Seas island, he signs aboard the *Pequod*, a whaling ship sailing out of Nantucket. The captain of the *Pequod* is the mysterious Ahab, unseen by his men for the first days of the voyage, who appears only to announce the purpose of their mission. They are out to hunt and kill the giant white sperm whale known as Moby Dick which, in an earlier voyage, had cost Ahab his leg. So determined is Ahab to destroy the white whale that he has brought on board his own private crew of expert harpooners. Nothing can deter Ahab from the quest and, as the ship sails on amid prophecies of doom and harbingers of evil to come, his lust for vengeance on Moby Dick only intensifies. When the whale is finally sighted, the scene is set for an epic confrontation which can only end in death and disaster. The novel is full of digressions and lengthy demonstrations of Melville's arcane knowledge (of the history of whaling, the biology of different species of whale, the mythology and meanings attached to the colour white and dozens of other subjects) but at its heart is a simple story of one man's doomed obsession. Ahab is a man possessed and it is his crazed pursuit of the white whale and its terrible outcome that, quite rightly, everybody remembers from the novel.

Film version: *Moby Dick* (directed by John Huston, with Gregory Peck as Ahab, 1956)

Read on

Billy Budd, Sailor; *Typee*
>> Joseph Conrad, *The Nigger of the Narcissus*; William Golding, *Rites of Passage*; >> Victor Hugo, *Toilers of the Sea*

READONATHEME: THE SEA

Erskine Childers, *The Riddle of the Sands*
>> Joseph Conrad, *Typhoon*
C.S. Forester, *A Ship of the Line*
Richard Hughes, *A High Wind in Jamaica*
Frederick Marryat, *Mr Midshipman Easy*
>> Herman Melville, *White-Jacket*

MARGARET MITCHELL (1900–49) USA

GONE WITH THE WIND (1936)

The American Civil War is the backdrop for Margaret Mitchell's panoramic lament for the lost glories of the American South and the story of headstrong beauty Scarlett O'Hara and her turbulent relationship with two men. When the book opens, just before the outbreak of hostilities, Scarlett is a spoilt teenage belle living on her family plantation, Tara, in Georgia. She is infatuated with the handsome son of a neighbouring plantation owner, Ashley Wilkes, but he marries another young woman, Melanie Hamilton. On the rebound, Scarlett weds Melanie's brother but she soon loses him to the war that has now begun and he dies in an outbreak of measles. As the war continues, her life becomes a struggle to survive and to retain and rebuild Tara, which is destroyed by the Yankee army. To achieve this goal she is prepared to do almost anything, from murdering a thief who threatens the plantation to marrying for the money to keep the place going. When the war finally ends, Scarlett renews her relationship with Rhett Butler, a caddish charmer whom she first met in the pre-war years and who helped her and Melanie escape the burning town of Atlanta during the fighting. When her second husband dies, she marries Rhett, who has long admired her feisty vitality, but happiness still eludes her. A huge bestseller when it first appeared (it still is) and the basis of one of the most famous of all Hollywood movies, *Gone with the Wind* was the only novel Mitchell published in her lifetime. (The manuscript of a short novel she wrote as a teenager was eventually discovered and published in the 1990s.) Few books have the sweeping power of this epic romance of ordinary lives caught up in the great events of history.

◀ **Film version:** *Gone With the Wind* (directed by Victor Fleming, starring Vivien Leigh as Scarlett and Clark Gable as Rhett Butler, 1939)

📚 Read on

Daphne Du Maurier, *Rebecca*; Colleen McCullough, *The Thorn Birds*; Alexandra Ripley, *Scarlett* (a sequel to Mitchell's novel, published in the 1990s)

WILLIAM MORRIS (1834–96) UK

NEWS FROM NOWHERE (1890)

William Morris was a man of prodigious and varied talents. As a craftsman and designer, he was one of the leading lights in the Arts and Crafts movements. As a poet, he wrote some of the most popular verse of the Victorian era. He was also a painter, a publisher and a polemicist for Socialist and Marxist ideas. Amid all the other frenetic creative activity with which he filled his life he also found time to produce several fantasy novels and works of utopian fiction which have influenced writers in the genre ever since. *News from Nowhere* is Morris's vision of a future England freed from the filth of its factories and slums. At the time he wrote the book, he was prominent in the Socialist League and it embodies his dream of what a truly socialist society might be. The narrator awakens in his Hammersmith house to find himself in a near-paradisal London of the early 21st century. Men and women live in freedom, work is a pleasure rather than a drudgery and central government has been abolished. The narrator travels through a dramatically changed city which Morris brings vividly to life. (Famously, the Houses of Parliament have been transformed into a dung market.) In the second part of the book, the narrator hears of the revolution that produced this utopia (it took place in 1952) and the novel concludes with a lovingly described journey up the Thames through a countryside returned to its pre-industrial beauty. Reading *News from Nowhere* today, with the benefit of hindsight on the 20th century, is a poignant and moving experience. How different the century was from Morris's utopian imaginings. Yet the book remains a powerful and vivid vision of how the world might be if we would only listen to the promptings of our better selves.

🐦 Read on

The Well at the World's End
Edward Bellamy, *Looking Backward*

READONATHEME: OTHER WORLDS/OTHER FUTURES

>> Samuel Butler, *Erewhon*
Anatole France, *Penguin Island*
Charlotte Perkins Gilman, *Herland*
James Hilton, *Lost Horizon*
Richard Jefferies, *After London*
David Lindsay, *A Voyage to Arcturus*
>> Jonathan Swift, *Gulliver's Travels*
>> H.G. Wells, *The Time Machine*
Yevgeni Zamyatin, *We*

FLANN O'BRIEN (1911–66) Ireland

AT SWIM-TWO-BIRDS (1939)

No précis can begin to do justice to the surreal complexity and comic playfulness of Flann O'Brien's masterpiece. The overall narrator of the book is an idle, hard-drinking student in Dublin who begins to write a novel about a novelist, Dermot Trellis, whose own fictional characters rebel against his tyranny. In a series of bewilderingly interlocking narratives, one hidden within another like Russian dolls, O'Brien creates a cavalcade of comic incident and a portrait gallery of weird characters. Figures from Irish legend like Finn McCool and King Sweeney appear to make their own contributions to the story, as do two American cowboys named Slug and Shorty, mysteriously plying their trade on the banks of the Liffey. Trellis creates a female character so beautiful he falls in love with her and forces himself upon her. She gives birth to a fully grown son who becomes one of the ringleaders in the plot to overthrow his father. O'Brien's sheer inventiveness is astonishing but nobody expecting a story which begins at the beginning and travels smoothly to a conclusion should pick up *At Swim-Two-Birds*. Flann O'Brien was the best-known pseudonym of Brian O'Nolan, an Irish civil servant, journalist and novelist. *At Swim-Two-Birds*, his first novel, was so unusual and offbeat that it very nearly wasn't published at all. Rejected by a number of publishers, it was finally seen by ›› Graham Greene who was working as a reader for another publishing firm and he recommended it strongly. When it was published, it won praise from other writers (›› James Joyce called O'Brien 'a real writer, with the true comic touch' and Dylan Thomas rather more bizarrely wrote in a review that the book was just the present 'to give your sister, if she's a loud, dirty, boozy girl') but failed to sell well. Today it's rightly recognized as both a masterpiece of modernist fiction and one of the funniest books of the 20th century.

📚 Read on

The Dalkey Archive; *The Third Policeman*
Samuel Beckett, *Murphy*; **»** James Joyce, *Ulysses*; Gilbert Sorrentino, *Mulligan Stew*

GEORGE ORWELL (1903–50) UK

ANIMAL FARM (1945)

Orwell's memorable political allegory is set at Manor Farm, run by a drunken and cruel farmer named Jones. Just before his death, one of the farm's pigs, the wise and elderly boar Old Major, tells the other animals of his vision of how the world might be if they were rid of Mr Jones and his exploitation. Inspired by Old Major's dream, the animals rise up and drive the humans from the farm. From now on, renamed Animal Farm, it is to be an ideal society working for the benefit of all the animals. All contact with humans will be avoided. Four legs will be good, two legs will be bad. At first all goes well and the two pig leaders of the revolution, Snowball and Napoleon, work together to make the farm successful and to see off Mr Jones when he returns to try to regain control. However, soon divisions occur in the leadership and the more ruthless of the two, Napoleon, wins out in the battle for command. Snowball is chased from the farm, rapidly becoming the scapegoat for all that begins to go wrong. All Old Major's dreams of a fairly run farm come to nothing and a new exploitation takes the place of the old. 'All animals are equal,' as the new slogan has it, 'but some animals are more equal than others'. The parallels between the events of *Animal Farm* and the real history of the Russian Revolution are exact (Napoleon, for example, is clearly meant to represent Stalin and Snowball Trotsky) but the book works as a dazzlingly inventive condemnation of any totalitarian system which begins with fine words and ends in tyranny. The moral of Orwell's fable remains valid long after the specific events it was satirizing have passed into the history books.

🎞 **Film version:** *Animal Farm* (animated version of the story, 1954)

📖 **Read on**
1984
Aesop, *The Complete Fables*; Andrey Platonov, *The Foundation Pit*; ››
Jonathan Swift, *Gulliver's Travels*

MARCEL PROUST (1871–1922) France

IN SEARCH OF LOST TIME (1913–27)

As the Monty Python team discovered in a famous comedy sketch, Proust's *In Search of Lost Time* is not an easy novel to summarize. Proust worked on it for more than a decade and it was published in seven volumes (three of them appearing posthumously). It is an epic tapestry of French society, particularly its upper echelons, told in the first person by a narrator named Marcel. Through Marcel's eyes, and across several decades, we see the lives of a group of rich socialites as they conduct their love affairs and friendships, gossip bitchily at parties, go to concerts and art exhibitions, react to the major events of the day (from the Dreyfus Affair to the First World War) and sense uneasily that their day is done and that their wealth and social position are on the wane. Marcel himself is an exquisitely sensitive narrator, acutely and ironically aware of the absurdity of much of the behaviour he observes so subtly, and open at all times to an appreciation of the transient beauty of both people and art. He is also preternaturally aware of the power of memory to shape our lives and to return us unexpectedly to the past. Famously, the novel begins with a long section in which the taste of a madeleine biscuit dipped in tea sends him back into his childhood and releases a stream of unconscious images from a world he has lost. *In Search of Lost Time* is a long, leisurely book (each volume is the size of an ordinary novel) and Proust's sentences often stretch languorously across the pages. Some people find his style irritating and the book unreadable. For others, *In Search of Lost Time*, as it slowly unfolds and moves backwards and forwards in time, is the greatest novel of the 20th century.

Film version: *Swann in Love* (with Jeremy Irons, 1983)

Read on

Jean Santeuil (Proust's first novel, abandoned when he was in his twenties but finally published 30 years after his death)

Alain-Fournier, *Le Grand Meaulnes*; Anthony Powell, *Dance to the Music of Time* (the most 'Proustian' sequence of novels in English); C.P. Snow, *Strangers and Brothers* (another long sequence of novels following the same characters through decades – much less sophisticated than Proust but interested in power and politics in a way that the French writer was not)

JOSEPH ROTH (1894–1939) Austria

THE RADETZKY MARCH (1932)

The First World War and the break-up of the vast, multi-cultural Hapsburg Empire into which he was born were the defining events in Roth's life. Plagued by chronic alcoholism and haunted by the sense of homelessness and alienation that years of exile in France and Germany brought, he returned time and again in his fiction to the world in which he grew up. Although he wrote brilliantly about Berlin in the troubled years of the Weimar Republic and about a Europe facing the twin threats of Fascism and Communism, his imagination was most deeply stirred by the past imperial glories that had been lost. His finest novel is **The Radetzky March**, which records the lives of three generations of a family in the declining decades of the Austro-Hungarian Empire, from defeat at the Battle of Solferino in the 1850s to the final rites administered by the events of the Great War. Joseph Trotta is raised from the level of lowly army lieutenant to privilege and greater social status when he saves the life of the Emperor Franz Joseph at Solferino but, as the years pass, his simple faith in the empire and its values is tarnished and compromised. He is, in the words of the novel, 'driven from the paradise of simple faith in Emperor and Virtue, Truth, and Justice' and, for his son and his grandson, the gap between the ideals of imperial service and the realities of the world grows ever larger. Roth uses the story of the Trottas as the central element in a melancholic panorama of a society in decline. The Trottas, and others like them, stagger, bewildered, into the 20th century and their poignant loss of faith in the empire that provided them with their privileges is captured by Roth with measured irony and great psychological insight.

🕮 Read on

Hotel Savoy; *Job*; *The Legend of the Holy Drinker*
Klaus Mann, *Mephisto*; Stefan Zweig, *Beware of Pity*

WALTER SCOTT (1771–1832) Scotland

THE HEART OF MIDLOTHIAN (1818)

Many of Scott's novels raid the real events of Scottish history for their settings and plots, and the action in *The Heart of Midlothian* begins with the Porteous Riots of 1736. These took place in Edinburgh after several people, part of a crowd gathered to witness an execution, were shot dead by the city guard, commanded by Captain John Porteous. Porteous was thought to have given the fatal orders without provocation and, when he was acquitted of wrongdoing, a mob dragged him from the Tolbooth prison – the Heart of Midlothian of Scott's title – and hanged him in the city's Grass Market. Into these genuine historical events Scott weaves his own story of the two half-sisters, Jennie and Effie Deans. Effie is the lover of George Staunton, one of the leaders of the rioters, and she herself is incarcerated in the Tolbooth where she awaits trial for the supposed murder of her illegitimate child. Jeanie has the opportunity to clear her sister's name but to do so would mean lying and she cannot bring herself to speak anything but the truth. Instead she sets out to walk to London to seek a royal pardon for Effie. On her journey she encounters Madge Wildfire, Staunton's former mistress, and her mother, who have kidnapped the child Effie is thought to have killed. The so-called Waverley novels (Scott wrote more than twenty, including such well-known titles as *Ivanhoe*, *Quentin Durward* and *Rob Roy*) were the bestsellers of their time and they more or less began the tradition of historical fiction which has continued to the present day. Enormously influential throughout Europe and America, they were imitated by many writers, from ➤➤ Dumas to Fenimore Cooper, and were adapted into countless theatrical and operatic versions during the 19th century. Today they have lost most of their popularity but *The Heart of Midlothian* is still a book that combines a compelling recreation of the past with characters whose human and moral dilemmas carry a lasting resonance.

⌕ Read on

Old Mortality; *Rob Roy*

James Fenimore Cooper, *The Last of the Mohicans* (the best-known novel by the writer sometimes known as 'the American Scott'); **»** Alexandre Dumas, *The Black Tulip*; **»** Victor Hugo, *The Hunchback of Notre Dame*; Alessandro Manzoni, *The Betrothed*; Charles Reade, *The Cloister and the Hearth*

READONATHEME: PAST HISTORIC

Ivo Andric, *The Bridge on the Drina*
» Charles Dickens, *A Tale of Two Cities*
Lloyd C. Douglas, *The Robe*
» Ford Madox Ford, *The Fifth Queen*
Robert Graves, *Count Belisarius*
Charles Kingsley, *Hereward the Wake*
» Sir Walter Scott, *Ivanhoe*
Henryk Sienkiewicz, *Quo Vadis?*
Lew Wallace, *Ben-Hur*
Mika Waltari, *The Egyptian*

JOHN STEINBECK (1902–68) USA

THE GRAPES OF WRATH (1938)

The novels of John Steinbeck, winner of the Nobel Prize for Literature in 1962, are surprisingly wide-ranging in their subject matter, from a Californian family saga (*East of Eden*) to a story of small-town resistance to the Nazis (*The Moon is Down*). He even produced his own version, posthumously published, of the story of King Arthur and the Knights of the Round Table. However, he is most often associated with tales of the Great Depression in America. His finest novel is *The Grapes of Wrath*, which records the sufferings of the Joad family as it is uprooted from its home in Oklahoma and heads for California in the hope of a new life. As the novel opens, Tom Joad has just been released from prison on parole and he makes his way back to the family farm, only to find that, after a ruinous crop failure, it has been repossessed by the banks who lent the Joads money. The family has no option now but to pile their few goods on to a truck and head out west. In doing so, they learn that they are like thousands of others who are making the same journey, seduced by the promise that jobs and the good life await them there. *The Grapes of Wrath* follows the family's trek to California and the gradual disillusionment that accompanies it. California is not the land of milk and honey they believed it to be. All the migrants, including the Joads, face exploitation by unscrupulous employers and, when they attempt to unite to combat that exploitation, they face violence and repression. Steinbeck's great novel is a moving and often tragic portrait of deprivation and hardship but it also reveals his belief in the power of ordinary people to cling to their humanity whatever they have to suffer.

🎞 **Film version:** *The Grapes of Wrath* (directed by John Ford, with Henry Fonda as Tom Joad, 1940)

📖 **Read on**

Cannery Row; *East of Eden*; *Of Mice and Men*

T.C. Boyle, ***The Tortilla Curtain*** (a tale of contemporary poverty and exploitation in which migrant Hispanic workers take the place of Steinbeck's Okies); Erskine Caldwell, ***Tobacco Road***; Jack London, ***Martin Eden***

STENDHAL (1783–1842) France

SCARLET AND BLACK (1830)

Julien Sorel is the son of a provincial carpenter but he is determined to rise in the world. His intelligence and his sexual attractiveness provide him with the means to do so. Sorel's hero is the fallen Napoleon but, in the new France of the restored Bourbon monarchs, talents other than military prowess are required. Julien is in training for the priesthood (despite spiritual doubts, he believes the church may offer him a career path to the fame and fortune he craves – the title alludes to the military and clerical lives that draw Sorel). He is taken into the household of Monsieur de Renal as a tutor, where he seduces his employer's wife and is eventually forced to leave to avert a scandal. Back in the seminary,

Julien is recommended to a position as personal secretary to a marquis and gets the opportunity to travel to the bright lights of Paris. Scandal threatens again when the marquis's daughter falls in love with him but her father, learning that she is pregnant with Julien's child, intervenes to ensure that the young man gains the noble title that will enable him to be a suitable husband for her. Julien has finally achieved the status in society that he has always believed to be his right but his past comes back to haunt him in the shape of Madame de Renal. Stendhal was the pen name used by the Swiss-born soldier and diplomat Henri-Marie Beyle, whose early career was shaped by his admiration for Napoleon (he was commissioned into the French army when still a teenager and served with the Emperor's headquarters staff on the disastrous invasion of Russia). His career as a writer only really began after Napoleon's downfall. *Scarlet and Black* (sometimes translated as *The Red and the Black*) is his finest work, a brilliant portrait of a self-invented adventurer and the society in which he attempts to rise.

📽 **Film versions:** *Le Rouge et le Noir* (1954); *The Scarlet and the Black* (1993, TV)

📖 **Read on**
The Charterhouse of Parma; *The Life of Henri Brulard*
>> Honoré de Balzac, *Lost Illusions*

LAWRENCE STERNE (1713–68) UK

TRISTRAM SHANDY (1760–7)

Sterne was an Irish-born clergyman who seemed destined for lifelong obscurity as a Yorkshire vicar until the publication of the first volumes of his book *The Life and Adventures of Tristram Shandy, Gentleman* in 1760 turned him into a literary celebrity in 18th-century London. *Tristram Shandy* is a novel like no other. The eponymous hero describes his own conception early in the book but he isn't actually born until a later volume. Nearly every page of the book provides the excuse for digressions and diversions on subjects that range from the science of military fortifications to the effect of names on human personality. Typographical tricks are scattered through the book. An all-black page mourns the death of one of the characters and a blank one is provided for the reader to create his or her own portrait of another. Within the eccentric narrative, which moves back and forth in time with often baffling rapidity, readers are introduced to the principal characters. Walter Shandy, Tristram's father, is a man with a thousand intellectual hobby-horses, willing at the drop of a hat to launch himself into lectures on the many, usually absurd theories in which he believes. Uncle Toby, Walter's brother, is a former soldier, suffering from a mysterious wound in the groin which hampers his courtship of the Widow Wadman. Together with the witty eccentric Parson Yorick (often seen as Sterne's self-portrait), Toby's servant Corporal Trim, the incompetent Dr Slop and the usually bemused Mrs Shandy, they inhabit a comic fictional world which is unique in English literature. Dr Johnson was dismissive of the book. 'Nothing odd will do long,' he is quoted as saying in Boswell's biography of him. '*Tristram Shandy* did not last.' For once, at least, Johnson was wrong. Not only has Sterne's work lasted, but as the years have passed, its innovative techniques and 'odd' devices have come to seem more and more like the inventions of a writer brilliantly anticipating the fiction of modernist novelists such as ➤➤ Joyce and ➤➤ Flann O'Brien.

🎬 Film version: *A Cock and Bull Story* (2006)

📖 Read on
A Sentimental Journey (a lightly fictionalized account of Sterne's travels in France and Italy)
➤➤ Miguel de Cervantes, *Don Quixote*; Denis Diderot, *Jacques the Fatalist*; Jan Potocki, *The Manuscript Found in Saragossa*; François Rabelais, *The Histories of Gargantua and Pantagruel*

ROBERT LOUIS STEVENSON (1850–94)
Scotland

THE STRANGE CASE OF DR JEKYLL AND MR HYDE (1886)
Stevenson's best-known works are chiefly historical adventure stories. *Treasure Island*, with its tale of pirates, treasure maps and a one-

legged ship's cook named Long John Silver, is usually taken to be a novel for children. *Kidnapped*, *Catriona* and *The Master of Ballantrae* raid Scottish history in the era of the Jacobite rebellions for stories of swash and buckle. Probably Stevenson's best and most challenging fiction, however, is his short novel, ***The Strange Case of Dr Jekyll and Mr Hyde***. Through a succession of cleverly interlocking narratives, Stevenson gradually reveals the truth behind the strange case. Dr Jekyll, convinced of the duality of man, has developed a drug which enables him to separate the good from the evil in his personality. The evil is embodied in the alter ego the drug releases, the morally repulsive Mr Hyde. At first Jekyll is able to move easily between the two personalities and Hyde is firmly under control but this does not last. Hyde begins to assert himself whether Jekyll wishes his appearance or not. Soon, Jekyll realizes to his horror, his transformation into Hyde will be permanent. Stevenson described ***The Strange Case of Dr Jekyll and Mr Hyde*** as 'a fine bogey tale' and certainly it has many of the elements of a traditional story of the supernatural but it also draws much of its power from the anxieties that lurked beneath the surface of Victorian society. Just how solid were the foundations of the civilization on which the era prided itself? Were rationality and morality merely veneers painted on the surface of much deeper and darker instincts? Stevenson's tale undermines the belief that vice and virtue can be easily distinguished and readily separated. Both Dr Jekyll and Mr Hyde lurk within us all and the refusal to acknowledge our dark side can only lead to tragedy.

◄ Film versions: *Dr Jekyll and Mr Hyde* (Fredric March in title roles, 1931); *Dr Jekyll and Mr Hyde* (Spencer Tracy in title roles, 1941); *The Two Faces of Dr Jekyll* (Paul Massie in title roles, 1960)

☞ **Read on**

The Suicide Club; *The Weir of Hermiston*

➤➤ Fyodor Dostoevsky, *The Double*; Daphne du Maurier, *The Scapegoat*;
➤➤ James Hogg, *The Private Memoirs and Confessions of a Justified Sinner*; Bram Stoker, *Dracula*; ➤➤ H.G. Wells, *The Invisible Man*

ITALO SVEVO (1861–1928) Austria/Italy

CONFESSIONS OF ZENO (1923)

Born in Trieste into a cosmopolitan family of Austro-Italian Jews, Ettore Schmitz worked for much of his life in a bank and in his father-in-law's paint business, writing only in his spare time and publishing his fiction at his own expense. In the 1890s, two novels (*A Life* and *As a Man Grows Older*) appeared under the pseudonym of Italo Svevo but they received little attention and the few readers they gained were puzzled by their oblique and ironic narratives. 'This incomprehension baffles me,' Schmitz/Svevo wrote plaintively and retreated into silence for the next quarter of a century. In 1907, he made what was to be the most important friendship of his life when he met the young ➤➤ James Joyce who was working as an English teacher in Trieste. Joyce encouraged the older man to believe in his writing and the result, years later, was the publication of *Confessions of Zeno*, the strange but compelling narrative of a man battling with his own neuroses and his addiction to tobacco. For Zeno Cosini, the 'last' cigarette is one that he regularly smokes from the moment he decides, as a young man, to give up his habit for health reasons. Many of the most important days of his life are marked by the smoking of a 'last' cigarette but it never is the last. Zeno's confessions take the shape of the journal he has been urged to keep by his psychoanalyst and in them he records not only his never-ending attempts to give up smoking but also his own, self-serving version of his relationships with his family, his business dealings, the progress of his marriage and his half-hearted affair with an aspiring singer. Idiosyncratic and unusual, *Confessions of Zeno* is an absorbing journey into one man's mind, with all its self-delusions and self-justifications. It is one of the great comic novels of the 20th century.

☙ Read on
A Life; *As a Man Grows Older*
>> Ivan Goncharov, *Oblomov*; >> James Joyce, *Portrait of the Artist as a Young Man*; Philip Roth, *Portnoy's Compaint*

JONATHAN SWIFT (1667–1745) UK/Ireland

GULLIVER'S TRAVELS (1726)
Born in Dublin to English parents, Swift divided his life between that city and London and between the acrimonious politics of the time and the

affairs of the Anglican church in Ireland. He was a prolific author of political pamphlets, satires and occasional verses but most of these appeared anonymously and the only work for which he was paid was the one which posterity has most admired – *Gulliver's Travels*. Often treated as a tale for children (and expurgated to make it more palatable as such), the voyages of Lemuel Gulliver provide a satirical view not just of the political and religious controversies of Swift's day but of the overweening pretensions of humankind through the ages. Gulliver, a ship's surgeon, is shipwrecked on Lilliput, an island where the inhabitants are only a few inches high. The Lilliputians are engaged in a war with a neighbouring island, Blefuscu, and Gulliver, potentially a giant weapon of mass destruction in this miniature world, is dragged unwillingly into it. When he refuses to assist in the complete subjugation of Blefuscu, the Lilliputians turn against him and it is only with the help of the Blefuscudans that he is able to escape home. The Lilliputians are what most people remember of *Gulliver's Travels* but they appear only in the first part of the book. In the rest of the book, Gulliver encounters other lands and other peoples, from the giant Brobdingnagians to the Houyhnhnms, equine philosophers who confirm Gulliver in his misanthropy and his horrified realization that he and his kind are little more than Yahoos, the filthy creatures over whom the Houyhnhnms have dominion. It is surprising that *Gulliver's Travels* won its place as a children's classic because it is an often bitter book, filled with Swift's caustic contempt for human vice and weakness. It remains, long after the particular political and religious disputes which provoked it have faded into history, the most biting and memorable of all English satires.

◄ **Film versions:** *The Three Worlds of Gulliver* (1959); *Gulliver's Travels* (1996, TV) (These and other film versions of the story, including a 1939 animated version, all lack the savage satire of the original.)

≋ **Read on**

›› Samuel Butler, *Erewhon*; ›› Voltaire, *Candide*

JUNICHIRO TANIZAKI (1886–1965) Japan

THE MAKIOKA SISTERS (1943–48)

Often described as Japan's greatest novelist of the 20th century, Tanizaki was a prolific writer, publishing his first book in his twenties and continuing to create challenging and disturbing fiction until he was an old man in his seventies. *Diary of a Mad Old Man*, published four years before his death, is the story of an elderly man's voyeuristic sexual obsession with his beautiful daughter-in-law and illustrates Tanizaki's lifelong interest in the erotic and in the often destructive power of sexuality. The other great subject of Tanizaki's fiction is Japan itself and the changes the 20th century imposed on its traditional culture. As a young man, Tanizaki was an enthusiastic advocate of greater westernization in his country but, from his thirties onwards, his books reflected his growing concerns that modernity was destroying all that was best in Japan. His greatest novel, *The Makioka Sisters*, is both a lament for the passing of a way of a life and a sophisticated, ironic and subtle study of the family which, in the novel, embodies it. Set in Osaka in the years leading up to the Second World War (the book began its serial publication during the war itself), *The Makioka Sisters* follows the fortunes of the four daughters of a once-wealthy and aristocratic family in decline. The sisters struggle to survive in a society that is changing around them. They cling to the rituals and refinement of the past but the future seems to hold no place for them. In the small dramas of their life – the attempts by the two older sisters to find a husband for the third, the fourth sister's rebellion against the constraints of tradition – Tanizaki finds the material for a sad and compelling saga of an old Japan under threat from the advent of the new.

⮂ Read on

The Key; *Some Prefer Nettles*
Yasunari Kawabata, *Snow Country*; Natsume Soseki, *Kokoro*

WILLIAM MAKEPEACE THACKERAY
(1811–63) UK

VANITY FAIR (1847–8)

Thackeray began his career as a writer of short satirical sketches and parodies but he turned to longer fiction in the 1840s, producing *The*

Memoirs of Barry Lyndon Esq, a picaresque tale of the eponymous narrator's progress in the world, in 1844, and *Vanity Fair* which was published in monthly parts in 1847 and 1848. The latter novel was his major achievement in fiction, as Thackeray himself recognized. Years later, passing down the street where he had been living when he wrote it, he joked with a friend. 'Down on your knees, you rogue, for here *Vanity Fair* was penned, and I will go down with you, for I have a high opinion of that little production myself.' That 'little production' is a huge panorama of Regency England that opens in Miss Pinkerton's Academy for Young Ladies in Chiswick where the two central female characters, Amelia Sedley and Becky Sharp, have finished their schooling and are about to depart for Amelia's house in town. The book follows the two friends as they make their way in the world. The kind and gentle Amelia marries George Osborne. Becky, lively, scheming and unscrupulous, marries Rawdon Crawley but is not above an intrigue with her friend's husband and is cast off by her own when Rawdon finds her entertaining the ageing rake Lord Steyne. George dies at the Battle of Waterloo and the pregnant Amelia is left to mourn his death. As the years pass, Becky makes her rackety progress through Regency society while Amelia, still cherishing the memory of George, lives in obscurity with her father and her son. Only when Becky finally reveals the truth about her relationship with George does Amelia turn to her faithful admirer Dobbin who has loved her from afar for many years. Both Becky's and Amelia's contrasting journeys through 'Vanity Fair', Thackeray's term (borrowed from *The Pilgrim's Progress*) for the worldly society he anatomizes so brilliantly, have reached their conclusions.

◤ **Film versions:** *Becky Sharp* (Hollywood adaptation, 1935); *Vanity Fair* (2004)

📚 **Read on**
Pendennis; *The History of Henry Esmond*
›› Charles Dickens, *David Copperfield*; ›› Henry Fielding, *Tom Jones*;
Tobias Smollett, *The Expedition of Humphrey Clinker*

LEO TOLSTOY (1828–1910) Russia

ANNA KARENINA (1878)

In his long life, Leo Tolstoy, born into a rich and aristocratic Russian family, took on many roles. At different times he was a soldier, seeing action in the Caucasus and the Crimea, an educational reformer who established schools for the peasant children on his estates, a Christian philosopher and, in his old age, a moral prophet and advocate of non-violence whose work was to influence people as diverse as Gandhi and Ludwig Wittgenstein. Most of all, he was a writer, whose works range from a trilogy of autobiographical fiction published in the 1850s (*Childhood*, *Boyhood* and *Youth*) to short stories, essays on the nature of art and expositions of his religious beliefs. His finest achievements are two of the greatest novels of the 19th century – *War and Peace* and *Anna Karenina*. Beginning with one of the most famous opening lines in all fiction ('Happy families are all alike; every unhappy family is unhappy in its own way'), *Anna Karenina* is the story of a beautiful and fashionable woman trapped in a loveless marriage with an older man, who seeks escape and fulfilment in an adulterous relationship with Count Vronsky, a dashing army officer. When Anna Karenina's husband, a dull and conventional bureaucrat and politician, discovers the affair, his principal concern is with the risk it poses to his own social position. Anna promises discretion but she becomes pregnant by Vronsky and the affair moves inexorably towards a tragic conclusion. Counterpointed with the affair between Anna and Vronsky is a parallel story of the courtship and eventual marriage – a successful one – between Kitty Scherbatskaya and the generous-hearted and compassionate intellectual Levin, a man in search of real meaning and significance in his life. The intertwined stories of the two different relationships are set against the background of a rich recreation of high society in Moscow and St. Petersburg and they come together to form one of the great masterpieces of social realism.

Film versions: *Anna Karenina* (Greta Garbo as Anna, 1935); *Anna Karenina* (Vivien Leigh as Anna, 1948); *Anna Karenina* (1997)

Read on
War and Peace
›› Gustave Flaubert, *Madame Bovary*; Nikolai Leskov, *Lady Macbeth of Mtsensk*; Boris Pasternak, *Dr Zhivago*; ›› Ivan Turgenev, *On the Eve*

WAR AND PEACE (1869)

Tolstoy's sweeping, panoramic portrait of Russia facing the crisis of Napoleon's invasion of the country is rightly considered one of the greatest novels ever written. Through the parallel and interconnected lives of three main characters, Tolstoy explores the effects of the war on them and all the people they know. Pierre Bezuhov, the illegitimate son of a wealthy aristocrat, is ill at ease and ungainly in the formal society of upper-crust St Petersburg and, as the novel opens, prefers boozy carousing with male companions to formal dinner parties where he feels a misfit. In search of meaning and direction in his life, Pierre is fated to endure much – a disastrous marriage to a beautiful fortune-hunter who betrays him with other men, a period of near-insanity during which he becomes convinced that he is destined to assassinate Napoleon – before he finds the consolation and redemption for which he spends most of the novel looking. Prince Andrei Bolkonsky, ambitious, patriotic and intelligent, fights with the Russian forces at the Battle of Austerlitz, where he is reported missing and is, for some time, assumed to be dead. When he returns to his estates, it is only to face the loss of his wife in childbirth and a political situation which, it becomes clear, will force him eventually to take up arms again. Natasha Rostov is the lively, spontaneous and charming daughter of a noble family who, in the course of the novel, is loved by both Pierre and Prince Andrei. One she inadvertently betrays through a misguided and temporary passion for a rakish wastrel, the other she finally marries. Focusing on the three central characters but opening out on to a vast canvas peopled by hundreds, *War and Peace* is a study of an entire society under pressure. All human life really is there.

🎞 **Film versions:** *War and Peace* (Hollywood version with Audrey Hepburn as Natasha and Henry Fonda as Pierre, 1956); *War and Peace* (an epic, eight-hour-long Russian adaptation, 1968)

📚 **Read on**
Anna Karenina
Vasily Grossman, *Life and Fate*; Mikhail Sholokhov, *And Quiet Flows the Don*; ➤➤ Stendhal, *Scarlet and Black*

ROBERT TRESSELL (1870–1911) Ireland

THE RAGGED TROUSERED PHILANTHROPISTS
(1914)

Robert Tressell's real name was Robert Noonan and he was born in Dublin. As a young man he emigrated to South Africa but returned to Europe around the turn of the century and spent the rest of his life as a painter and decorator, working at his writing in his spare time. First appearing posthumously (it had been rejected by several publishers during his lifetime), Tressell's only novel is the story of a group of painters and decorators in Edwardian England and the attempts by the hero Frank Owen to rouse their political awareness and to end their exploitation by the state and by their employers. Set in the fictional town of Mugsborough (a disguised version of Hastings, where Tressell had himself lived and worked), the book is a scathing indictment of the way society operates. The philanthropists of the title are, of course, the workers themselves who, despite the poverty reflected in their ragged trousers, continue to give their labour for low wages and to acquiesce in their own exploitation. Tressell exposes the hypocrisy and corruption of the 'better' classes in town who mouth clichés of Christian virtue while continuing to support a status quo that subverts the fundamental principles of Christianity. As much of his anger, though, expressed through the speeches of Owen, seems to be directed against the workers and their wilful refusal, as he sees it, to recognize where their own interests lie. Owen's fellows are as likely to mock his idealism and his eloquent denunciations as to listen to him. Poignant and comic by turns, *The Ragged Trousered Philanthropists* has probably inspired more British socialists than the complete works of Marx ever did and it remains a wonderfully vivid and lively novel – the finest work of genuinely working-class fiction ever published.

🕮 Read on

Walter Greenwood, *Love on the Dole*; ›› George Orwell, *Keep the Aspidistra Flying*; ›› H.G. Wells, *The History of Mr Polly*

ANTHONY TROLLOPE (1815–82) UK

THE WARDEN (1855)

'Three hours a day will produce as much as a man ought to write,' Trollope noted in his *Autobiography*. If we assume that he followed his own precept, Trollope must have made good use of his three hours because he published 47 novels together with volumes of short stories, travel books and even a biography of the Roman orator and politician, Cicero. Of his novels, the best-loved are the Barsetshire books, set in his invented rural county in the west of England. In the first of the series, *The Warden*, the elderly clergyman Septimus Harding is appointed by the Bishop of Barchester, the cathedral city of the county, to be the warden of an almshouse. Mr Harding is too unworldly to notice that the funding of the almshouse is a potential scandal but others are not. Voices are raised, including that of his daughter's suitor, against the misuse of church money and the battle lines between reformers and conservatives are drawn up. The unfortunate Mr Harding is caught in the middle. Trollope followed *The Warden* with five further novels in the 'Chronicles of Barsetshire', published over the next twelve years. Of these, the most popular is undoubtedly *Barchester Towers*, which includes the character of Mrs Proudie, the domineering and interfering wife of the newly appointed Bishop of Barchester, one of the most memorable figures in Victorian fiction. The best is probably *The Last Chronicle of Barset*, a subtle and moving study of a church scandal and the proud, self-righteous clergyman at its centre. The novels can all be read individually but they are a series with recurring characters (*The Last Chronicle of Barset* sees the contrasting deaths of Mr Harding and

Mrs Proudie) and readers are well advised to introduce themselves to the charms of Barsetshire with *The Warden*.

➲ Read on

Barchester Towers; *The Last Chronicle of Barset*
Barbara Pym, *Some Tame Gazelle*; Angela Thirkell, *High Rising* (in the 1930s Thirkell wrote a series of novels which she set in her own version of Trollope's Barsetshire and this is the first)

THE WAY WE LIVE NOW (1875)

Trollope is often imagined to be a novelist who wrote nothing but cosy narratives of intrigue and preferment in the cathedral close. In fact, he was as scathing a critic of high Victorian complacency as ➤➤ Dickens and a writer with a brilliant eye for the ways in which power and wealth corrupt the people who possess them. As a satirical panorama of 19th-century London, there is no novel to match Trollope's masterpiece, *The Way We Live Now*. At the heart of the book's unblinkered analysis of the power of money to shape society is the mysterious financier, Augustus Melmotte, who emerges, apparently from nowhere, to become one of the country's great and good. Investors fall over themselves to throw cash at his companies, impoverished aristocrats seek to ingratiate themselves with him (one even hopes to marry her son to his daughter) and, elected to parliament, he becomes one of the nation's legislators. Melmotte's success, however, is a mirage and his fortunes are built on sand. When the precarious edifice of his finances comes crashing to the ground, fair weather friends desert him in droves and he is left to contemplate the ruin of his life. Around the figure of Melmotte dance the dozens of other characters who populate this ambitious and absorbing book. 'I was instigated by what I conceived to be the commercial profligacy of the age,' Trollope wrote of his motivation in writing *The Way We Live Now* and the novel is a magisterial indictment of the moral bankruptcy of mid-Victorian England. From the inner workings of government to the jealousies and intrigues of the literary world, from the dodgy dealings of shady companies to the ambivalent relationship between Old World aristocracy and New World money, Trollope turns a cold, satirical eye on the institutions of his times and finds them all lacking.

📖 Read on

Can You Forgive Her? (the first of the Palliser series which depict the world of Victorian politics and high society)

›› Charles Dickens, *Our Mutual Friend*; John Galsworthy, *The Forsyte Saga*; ›› William Makepeace Thackeray, *Vanity Fair*

IVAN TURGENEV (1818–83) Russia

FATHERS AND SONS (1861)

Arkady is a young student who returns home to his country estate together with his much-admired friend Bazarov. Bazarov is a man of strong and outspoken views, a charismatic figure who can impress even those, like Arkady's father, who reject his opinions. Yet Bazarov finds difficulty in applying his intellectual convictions to the messy realities of life. His 'love' affair with Madame Odintsova is a catalogue of misunderstandings and missed opportunities, far removed from the philosophy of free love he espouses. A quarrel with Arkady's uncle Pavel ends in a ludicrous duel. When Bazarov returns to his own estate, his mind preoccupied, he finds himself in the midst of a typhus epidemic and, in tending the victims of it, he contracts the disease himself and dies. As its title suggests, the struggle between the generations is at the heart of *Fathers and Sons*. Its most memorable character, Bazarov, rejects what he sees as the failed romanticism of the older generation in favour of radical new ideas but these too are seen to be fatally flawed. His life appears to have been a failure and his early death bitterly ironic proof of his belief in the essential futility of the world but it is clear that his powerful personality has had its effect on most of the other characters in the novel. *Fathers and Sons*, Turgenev's most famous book, was widely admired in Western Europe during his lifetime and Turgenev, who spent long periods of his life in Germany and France, was the Russian novelist closest in spirit to contemporary Western writers such as ❯❯ Flaubert, whom he knew well. In Russia, his work has often been overshadowed by the novels of writers like ❯❯ Tolstoy and ❯❯ Dostoevsky, seen as somehow more authentically 'Russian' than Turgenev, but his coolly ironic and humane vision of the world, exemplified by *Fathers and Sons*, is worth discovering.

🕮 Read on
A House of Gentlefolk; *On the Eve*

>> Gustave Flaubert, *Sentimental Education*; L.P. Hartley, *The Go-Between*

MARK TWAIN (1835–1910) USA

THE ADVENTURES OF HUCKLEBERRY FINN (1884)

According to Ernest Hemingway, 'All modern American literature comes from one book by Mark Twain called *Huckleberry Finn*'. Mark Twain was the pseudonym of Samuel Langhorne Clemens who took as his *nom de plume* a cry heard on the Mississippi from men measuring the depth of the river ('mark twain' meant the river was two fathoms deep) and first made his reputation as a writer and humourist with a travel book entitled *The Innocents Abroad*, published in 1869. *The Adventures of Tom Sawyer* was published in 1876 and the novel which Hemingway believed to be so seminal appeared eight years later. Huckleberry Finn had appeared as a major character in *The Adventures of Tom Sawyer*, eventually rescued from his life as the outcast son of the town drunk and adopted by a kind-hearted elderly lady whose life he saved. In the later novel, he tells his own story, in his own distinctive voice, of what happens to him after he has been taken in by the Widow Douglas. His boozy father reappears in his life and reclaims him but, weary of Pap's brutality, Huck fakes his own death (he kills a pig to provide the necessary blood) and escapes. He then joins forces with the runaway slave

Jim and they take a raft down the Mississippi where encounters with thieves, fellow vagabonds, larger-than-life con-artists and slave-catchers await them. *The Adventures of Huckleberry Finn* is open to many interpretations – at one level it is simply a series of light-hearted and very funny picaresque adventures – but its importance to later literature, highlighted by Hemingway, lies in the way it embodies so brilliantly two contrasting urges in American life and American literature. Widow Douglas's desire to 'sivilize' Huck and his own wish to escape this fate and 'to light out for the territory' represent the need to tame the wilderness and the longing for freedom to roam it that have regularly been at the heart of much of the best American fiction.

 Film versions: *The Adventures of Huckleberry Finn* (with Mickey Rooney, 1939); *The Adventures of Huck Finn* (with Elijah Wood, 1993)

 Read on
The Adventures of Tom Sawyer; Pudd'n'head Wilson

SIGRID UNDSET (1882–1949) Norway

KRISTIN LAVRANDSDOTTER (1920–2)
Winner of the Nobel Prize for Literature in 1928, the Norwegian writer Sigrid Undset had published her most significant novel in three

volumes earlier that decade. *Kristin Lavrandsdotter* is an epic historical fiction, set in Norway in the Middle Ages, which follows the eponymous heroine from her youth to her old age. Undset was the daughter of a well-known archaeologist and her interest in the past began when she was a small girl. She later cited her childhood reading of the Old Norse sagas as 'the most important turning point in my life' and her finest novel has some of the elemental quality of the medieval stories she so admired. It is also a book that finds the concerns and anxieties of the 20th century – political, spiritual and sexual – reflected in the distant mirror of the 14th century. This is not historical fiction as escapist literature. In the first of the three volumes, *The Wreath*, readers see Kristin as a young woman and watch her break her betrothal to another man in order to pursue her passionate relationship with the attractive but irresponsible Erlend Nikolausson. In the second volume, *The Wife*, she is married to Erlend and obliged to shoulder the responsibilities of motherhood and the management of his estate, as he strives to make his way in the brutal politics of the era. The trilogy concludes with *The Cross* in which Kristin, estranged from Erlend, faces the destruction of her world with the coming of the Black Death. *Kristin Lavrandsdotter* is one of the greatest of all works of historical fiction, a novel conceived on a gigantic scale which succeeds both as a remarkable evocation of the past in which it is set and as a record of one vividly created character's progress through life.

📖 Read on

Jenny (an early work of social realism); *The Master of Hestviken* (another giant work of historical fiction, set in medieval Scandinavia)

➤➤ Halldór Laxness, *Iceland's Bell*; Martin Anderson Nexo, *Pelle the Conqueror*

VOLTAIRE (1694–1778) France

CANDIDE (1759)

In his day François Marie Arouet – universally known as Voltaire – was the embodiment of the philosophical beliefs of the Enlightenment and one of the most famous men in Europe. He was renowned as a dramatist, poet, historian and political thinker. Today he is best remembered for his satirical novellas, especially *Candide*. The book tells the story of the naïve and gentle young Candide, schooled by his tutor Dr Pangloss in the optimistic philosophy that 'all is for the best in this, the best of all possible worlds', who discovers in his travels around 18th-century Europe and South America that the Panglossian doctrine leaves much to be desired. When he is caught kissing his guardian's daughter and is expelled from the seclusion of the castle where he has spent his childhood, he soon finds that the world is a much more wicked place than he imagines. He witnesses the brutalities of war at first hand. He travels to Lisbon in the aftermath of the 1755 earthquake there and sees that the acts of God can be as terrible, if not more so, than the acts of man. Religion, in the shape of the Jesuits and the Inquisition, offers few if any comforts. Travelling to the New World,

Candide and his love Cunégonde, learn that cruelty, greed and hypocrisy are as common there as they are in the Old World. Only in the utopian land of Eldorado, briefly visited by Candide, does virtue reign. And, after all his trials and tribulations, only in a simple life led close to nature, can he and Cunégonde find happiness. Intended as a mordant satire on the more ludicrously optimistic philosophical ideas of his day, Voltaire's fable of innocence abroad in a violent world has become much more than that. It is a clear-eyed, ruthlessly unsentimental assault on all those who insist that the world is other than it is.

☙ Read on
Zadig
Samuel Johnson, *The History of Rasselas*; Baron de Montesquieu, *Persian Letters*; ›› Jonathan Swift, *Gulliver's Travels*

EVELYN WAUGH (1903–66) UK

A HANDFUL OF DUST (1934)
In his satiric fantasies of Bright Young Things in 1920s Mayfair, books like *Decline and Fall* and *Vile Bodies*, Evelyn Waugh captured a hedonistic world of parties and pleasure-seeking with cruel and exaggerated comedy. In his later career, metropolitan decadence no longer held quite the fascination it had had for him when he was

younger and novels like *Brideshead Revisited* and the volumes which make up the *Sword of Honour* trilogy, while still very funny, are self-consciously serious attempts to chart the decline of an aristocratic, and specifically Catholic, way of life that he believed finer and more humane than the society which overwhelmed it. In *A Handful of Dust*, Waugh wrote a novel that is poised between farce and tragedy, full of the cruel social satire that characterizes his first fiction and yet marked by an awareness of the real pains that his characters endure. Tony Last is the impoverished owner of a country house forced to endure both the death of his son in a hunting accident and the adultery of his wife, Brenda, who conducts an affair with a parasitic man-about-town named John Beaver. At first, Last agrees to divorce his wife but, learning that this might put his house and estate at jeopardy, he changes his mind and refuses to cooperate. Instead he heads off on a wild trip to the Amazonian jungle in an attempt to forget his troubles where, as back home the affair between Brenda and Beaver peters out, he is doomed to one of the more bizarre fates to befall any character in English fiction. Waugh's caricatures of the social butterflies and idle adulterers of upper-class London life are as sharp and comic as ever but *A Handful of Dust* indicates a deepening of his bitter, and ultimately pessimistic, views of the changes in English society.

🕮 Read on

Brideshead Revisited; *Decline and Fall*; *Scoop*
Nancy Mitford, *The Pursuit of Love*; Anthony Powell, *Afternoon Men*

H.G. WELLS (1866–1946) UK

KIPPS (1905)

Wells, the son of a professional cricketer turned unsuccessful tradesman, escaped the lower middle-class drudgery that might have been his lot by winning a scholarship to the Normal School of Science in Kensington, London (now Imperial College) where one of his teachers was the famous biologist and disciple of Darwin, T.H. Huxley. His first novels, published in the 1890s, were the 'scientific romances' such as *The Time Machine* and *The War of the Worlds*, which are still his best-known works and which created his reputation as the founding father of science fiction. But Wells also wrote a series of novels which drew on his knowledge of the lives and dreams of the classes from which he came. The best of these is ***Kipps***. Subtitled 'The Story of a Simple Soul', the novel charts the changing fortunes of its central character, Arthur Kipps, who learns at first hand the realities of both poverty and riches in Edwardian England. An orphan raised by his aunt and uncle, Kipps experiences dreary years as a draper's apprentice before unexpected news of a large legacy changes his life. Kipps is now a 'gentleman' and, in the bitterest comedy of the book, he sees for himself the difference that money can make. Those who had once scorned him are now only too keen to befriend him but Kipps's new-found wealth brings him little satisfaction and much social humiliation. Only when he follows the dictates of his own heart and courts and marries his childhood sweetheart does he find happiness. After a series of further ups and downs on life's ladder he is left to reflect 'what a rum go everything is' and that 'I don't suppose there ever was a chap like me'. Touching and comic, Wells's portrait of his amiable hero and his voyage through the treacherous waters of the English class system remains a novel to be cherished.

🞂 **Film version:** *Kipps* (directed by Carol Reed, with Michael Redgrave as Kipps, 1941)

⮂ Read on
The History of Mr Polly; *Tono-Bungay*
>> Charles Dickens, *Great Expectations*; >> George Orwell, *Coming Up for Air*; J.B. Priestley, *The Good Companions*

EDITH WHARTON (1862–1937) USA

THE HOUSE OF MIRTH (1905)
Born into a wealthy and socially prominent New York family, Edith Newbold Jones married the Boston banker Edward Wharton when she was in her twenties. Although she had written stories from her girlhood, it was not until she was in her late thirties that she began to publish her work. For the next 40 years she produced fiction in a range of styles, from grim tragedies set in rural New England (*Ethan Frome*, for example) to atmospheric ghost stories, but her greatest books examine, with a cool but jaundiced eye, the social conventions of the

upper-class New York society with which she was most familiar. *The House of Mirth*, perhaps the finest instance of her most characteristic work, follows the social decline of its heroine, Lily Bart, who begins the book as the house guest of wealthy relatives and, by the end, is forced to the desperate expedient of taking a job as a milliner. In the interim she has had opportunities to marry and secure her future but she has, for a variety of reasons, either lost them or turned them down. One potential husband, the pious heir to a large fortune, is dismayed when she refuses to spend her Sunday in church. Another fails to win her because Lily considers him insufficiently well off. Her actions come back to haunt her as she falls further and further down the social scale. Eventually a woman who was once beautiful and elegant is reduced, through a combination of her own bad decisions and the malevolent gossip of others, to impoverished gentility and the realization that her life has been a failure. Wharton is remorselessly clear-sighted both about the values of the society in which Lily lives and about the marriage market which ultimately decides her fate.

🖿 **Film version:** *The House of Mirth* (with Gillian Anderson as Lily Bart, 2000)

🕮 **Read on**
The Age of Innocence; *Ethan Frome*
Louis Auchinloss, *The House of Five Talents*; William Dean Howells, *The Rise of Silas Lapham*; ❯❯ Henry James, *The Europeans*

OSCAR WILDE (1854–1900) Ireland

THE PICTURE OF DORIAN GRAY (1891)

Oscar Wilde's spectacular fall from grace, his sudden plunge from fêted author of epigrammatic comedies like *The Importance of Being Earnest* to prisoner in Reading Gaol, is one of the best-known and most tragic stories in the history of literature. At Wilde's trials, much was made of his artistic beliefs, assumed to have a direct link to what was seen as his sexual immorality. In the preface to his only novel, *The Picture of Dorian Gray*, he asserted that, 'There is no such thing as a moral or an immoral book. Books are well written or badly written. That is all.' It was a statement that came back to haunt him. The story to which it is attached is a Faustian account of a young man who, unaware, sells his soul to retain his youth and beauty. Dorian Gray is a handsome and well-connected young man who, as the novel opens, is sitting for a portrait by the painter Basil Hallward. Tempted by the hedonistic philosophy of Lord Henry Wotton, Mephistopheles to Dorian's Faust, who believes that youth and pleasure are the only good things in life, Dorian expresses the wish that the portrait might suffer the ravages of ageing while he retains his looks. His wish is granted and, over the next eighteen years, as he plunges further into vice, cruelty and even murder, he keeps his beauty while the painting, hidden away, bears all the marks of his sins. Ironically, given his statement in the preface, Wilde produced in *The Picture of Dorian Gray* a work which virtually demands to be read as a moral fable. Dorian appears to have escaped retribution for his many sins ... but not forever. 'All art is quite useless,' Wilde also states in the preface to the book but perhaps Dorian's portrait is the exception that proves his rule.

📽 **Film version:** *The Picture of Dorian Gray* (1945)

📖 **Read on**

J.K. Huysmans, *Against Nature*; ›› Robert Louis Stevenson, *The Strange Case of Dr Jekyll and Mr Hyde*

P.G. WODEHOUSE (1881–1975) UK

RIGHT HO, JEEVES (1934)

Over more than 70 years and nearly a hundred books, P.G. Wodehouse created his own parallel universe of lovelorn silly asses, formidable middle-aged aunts and eccentric aristocrats. His greatest creations were the amiable but slightly dim-witted man about town Bertie Wooster and his imperturbable, resourceful and super-intelligent 'gentleman's gentleman', Jeeves, who appeared together in more than a dozen novels and collections of short stories. *Right Ho, Jeeves*, one of the best of the series, finds Bertie drawn into the tangled love life of his old school chum, teetotal bachelor and newt-fancier Gussie Fink-Nottle. Gussie is a shy young man who has fallen for a drippy girl named Madeline Bassett but is too tongue-tied whenever he is with her to tell her how he feels. He recruits Bertie to inform Madeline of his adoration but much confusion ensues when she imagines that Bertie is speaking on his own behalf rather than his chum's. As Wodehouse's usual convoluted but brilliantly organized plot moves towards its eventual resolution, other would-be lovers face misunderstandings and broken engagements, Bertie's Aunt Dahlia sees her household descend into chaos and Gussie, fired up by an unaccustomed drinking bout, wreaks havoc at a school prize-giving ceremony. Only the genius of Jeeves can restore order and bring the assorted couples together. ▸▸ Evelyn Waugh wrote of Wodehouse that his 'idyllic world can never stale. He will continue to release future generations from captivity that may be more irksome than our own. He has made a world for us to live in and delight in.' As Waugh realized, the great strength of Wodehouse's fiction and the reason it continues to charm new generations of readers is that he created a fantasy universe which can never date because it never existed. Jeeves and Wooster are at the heart of that universe and *Right Ho, Jeeves* sees them in their prime.

ಲ Read on

The Code of the Woosters; *Leave it to Psmith*; *Uncle Fred in the Springtime*
E.M. Delafield, *The Diary of a Provincial Lady*; ▸▸ Stella Gibbons, *Cold Comfort Farm*; Jerome K. Jerome, *Idle thoughts of an Idle Fellow*

READONATHEME: COMIC CLASSICS

Anon (Henry Howarth Bashford), *Augustus Carp, Esq., By Himself*

Max Beerbohm, *Zuleika Dobson*

E.F. Benson, *Mapp and Lucia*

George and Weedon Grossmith, *The Diary of a Nobody*

Jerome K. Jerome, *Three Men in a Boat*

Stephen Leacock, *Sunshine Sketches of a Little Town*

Barry Pain, *The Eliza Stories*

>> P.G. Wodehouse, *The Mating Season*

VIRGINIA WOOLF (1882–1941) UK

MRS DALLOWAY (1925)

Clarissa Dalloway, a London society hostess, is preparing for an evening party. An old suitor, Peter Walsh, has returned from a long absence in India and awakened memories of her past and of the choices which have shaped her life. Beneath her conventional exterior, more romantic impulses and more poignant regrets lurk than her outward persona might suggest and Woolf's fluid, impressionistic narrative of the day's events allows space for these to emerge. Clarissa's story is counterpointed by that of Septimus Smith, a disturbed veteran of the Great War, who wanders London, his distressed wife in tow, imagining messages aimed at himself in the ordinary events of a city day. An aeroplane sky-writing advertising slogans has news for him, the birds in Regent's Park are speaking to him in Ancient Greek, the dogs there are metamorphosing alarmingly into men. Mrs Dalloway and Septimus Smith never meet but the novel concludes with the party she has been planning all day and there she hears, in passing, that he has committed suicide. Although the action of the novel all takes place on the one day, Virginia Woolf's use of interior monologue and memory opens up the narrative to longer perspectives. Mrs Dalloway's own earlier life and the dreadful experiences of Septimus Smith in the war are palpable presences in the novel even if readers are shown them only indirectly. In the years after Mrs Dalloway, Woolf went on to write other novels (*To the Lighthouse*, *The Waves*) which were even more adventurous in technique and which established her as one of Britain's leading exponents in literary modernism. However, the earlier novel is neatly positioned between the more conventional style of her first books and the demanding experimentation, often difficult to read, of her later work. It has many claims to being her finest novel.

🕮 Read on

To the Lighthouse; *The Waves*
Michael Cunningham, *The Hours*; Dorothy Richardson, *Pilgrimage* (a massive, multi-volume novel sequence by a contemporary of Woolf which uses many of the same stream of consciousness techniques)

ÉMILE ZOLA (1840–1902) France

GERMINAL (1885)

The son of an Italian engineer, Zola was born in Paris and began his career as a journalist. As a novelist, he became the leading figure in French naturalism and embarked on a massive survey of late 19th-century life in his Rougon-Macquart novels, so-called because of the names of the two families whose varying fortunes are at the heart of the sequence. *Germinal*, the thirteenth novel in the Rougon-Macquart series, is set in the coalfields of northern France and its central character is Étienne Lantier, a young worker forced to take a job in the pits. Radicalized by his experience of the suffering and exploitation of the miners, Étienne becomes a socialist and a fiery advocate of the workers' rights. When the miners are threatened with wage cuts he becomes one of the leaders of the strike called in protest. As the strike drags on, the workers become increasingly desperate and hungry and eventually rioting breaks out which is savagely repressed by the authorities. Étienne watches in despair as his fellow-miners are eventually forced to return to work but Souvarine, one of the more violent of the strikers, has plans to sabotage the mine. *Germinal* is unrelenting and uncompromising in revealing the hellish conditions in which the miners work and in depicting the ruthless suppression of their attempts to improve them. There are few better portraits in literature of the brutal realities of class conflict. However, Zola was a novelist not a social scientist, and his emphasis is as much on the individuals caught up in the strike (the idealistic, fierce-tempered Étienne, his friend, the ageing miner Maheu, Maheu's daughter

Catherine) as it is on the abstract social forces that shape their lives. More than a century after the book was published its characters and their desperate struggles to survive can still touch and move readers profoundly.

📽 Film versions: *Germinal* (1963); *Germinal* (starring Gérard Depardieu, 1993)

📖 Read on
La Bête Humaine; *Nana*; *Thérèse Raquin* (two lovers murder the woman's husband but descend into a hell of their own making)
Theodore Dreiser, *An American Tragedy*; W. Somerset Maugham, *Liza of Lambeth* (Maugham's first novel was a conscious effort to match in English literature the naturalism of French novelists like Zola); ▶▶ Guy de Maupassant, *A Life: The Humble Truth*

INDEX